Windows® XP KillerTips

Kleber Stephenson

D1216163

WINDOWS XP® KILLER TIPS

The Windows XP
Killer Tips Team

EDITOR
Barbara E. Thompson

TECHNICAL EDITOR
Tommy Maloney

PROOFREADER
Richard Theriault

PRODUCTION EDITOR
Kim Gabriel

PRODUCTION
Dave Damstra
Dave Gales
Ted LoCascio
Margie Rosenstein

COVER DESIGN AND
CREATIVE CONCEPTS
Felix Nelson

SITE DESIGN
Stacy Behan

The New Riders Team

PUBLISHER
David Dwyer

ASSOCIATE PUBLISHER
Stephanie Wall

EXECUTIVE EDITOR
Steve Weiss

PRODUCTION MANAGER
Gina Kanouse

PROJECT EDITOR
Jake McFarland

PROOFREADER
Gloria Schurick

PRODUCTION
Wil Cruz

PUBLISHED BY
New Riders Publishing

Copyright © 2003 by Kleber Stephenson

International Standard Book Number: 0-7357-1357-X

Library of Congress Catalog Card Number: 2002117491

06 05 04 03   7 6 5 4 3 2

Interpretation of the printing code: The rightmost double-digit number is the year of the book's printing; the rightmost single-digit number is the number of the book's printing. For example, the printing code 03-1 shows that the first printing of the book occurred in 2003.

Composed in Myriad, Trebuchet, and Helvetica by NAPP Publishing

Printed in the United States of America

Trademarks
All terms mentioned in this book that are known to be trademarks or service marks have been appropriately capitalized. New Riders Publishing cannot attest to the accuracy of this information. Use of a term in the book should not be regarded as affecting the validity of any trademark or service mark.

Windows is a registered trademark of Microsoft Corporation.

Warning and Disclaimer
This book is designed to provide information about Windows XP tips. Every effort has been made to make this book as complete and as accurate as possible, but no warranty of fitness is implied.

This information is provided on an as-is basis. The authors and New Riders Publishing shall have neither liability nor responsibility to any person or entity with respect to any loss or damages arising from the information contained in this book or from the use of the discs or programs that may accompany it.

www.newriders.com
www.windowsxpkillertips.com

For my wonderful wife, Debbie

and amazing children, Jarod and Jenna

ACKNOWLEDGMENTS

This book would never have been possible if it weren't for the support and understanding of my family and friends. I simply couldn't have done it without them. I'm so grateful to everyone. Thanks!

I first want to thank God, Jesus Christ; my life has been so wonderfully blessed and I feel Him in my life every day. Thanks for always being there for me and always listening to my prayers. Next, I want to thank my wife, Debbie. You're simply the most beautiful woman I've ever seen; you have the most amazing smile. You're my best friend, a fantastic mother, and you completely crack me up (all the time). I still can't believe that I was lucky enough to marry you. I love you more every day.

I also want to thank my children, Jarod and Jenna. Just thirty seconds with you guys and I realize how great my life truly is. You make every single day better. I'm so proud of both of you; you're definitely my greatest accomplishment. Jarod, you're so confident and self-assured, and the most interesting person I've ever met. There's no one I'd rather just hang out with. Jenna, you have your mother's beauty and even at age two, you're already so charming and sweet that you preoccupy everyone in a room and immediately steal their hearts. You stole mine the moment you were born. Thanks guys, for reminding me when I'm ignoring you and for not letting me get away with it.

Thanks also to my parents, Kleber and Barbara. I don't have enough pages in this book to express my gratitude for my mother. I wish everyone could have a mother as wonderful, as caring, and as giving as she is. Everything that's good in me I got from her. And Dad, thanks for showing me that there's no substitute for enthusiasm, and for the mantra, "It just doesn't get any better than this!" I agree Dad—it doesn't. And to the best sisters anyone could ever have: Cheryl, Kalebra, Julie, and Heidi; the four of you make our family great. I'm completely blown away to see how successful you've all become. You're all incredible! Thanks for your support and encouragement!

I also want to thank my grandmother, Reverend Ethel Trice—the most influential person I've ever known. She'd always get me to follow the right path even though I was determined not to. She taught me that I could do anything. She's no longer with us, but the world's a much better place because she was once with us. I miss her.

In addition, I'd like to express my tremendous appreciation and gratitude for my staff at Medical Assisted Services and U.S. Diginet—a fantastic team that gives its best each and every day. Everyone should be so fortunate to work with such a great group of people.

Of course, a very special thanks to Scott Kelby—you're simply the coolest, and an inspiration. And to my sister Kalebra. Ever since we were little kids hanging out in the trees in our backyard hoarding candy and cracking jokes, I've thought you were the greatest, and I still think you're the greatest. I'd like also to thank everyone at KW Media Group, especially Barbara Thompson, Felix Nelson, Tommy Maloney, Kim Gabriel, Dave Damstra, Dave Gales, and Margie Rosenstein. I couldn't possibly imagine a better production team to work with. All of you made producing this book seem effortless.

Finally, I'd like to thank my "PC Posse" (people who know a lot more about computers than I do), especially Steve Iverson and Larry Brown. I've known Steve for more than a decade, and he's taught me more about computers (by fixing my screw-ups) than anyone I've ever known. Larry, you're scary (couldn't resist); if the Government knew about you, you'd either be working for them, or you'd be in jail.

Again, many, many thanks to everyone!

ABOUT THE AUTHOR

Kleber Stephenson

Kleber is President of U.S. Diginet—Interactive Communications, an award-winning, full-service provider of Internet solutions, integrated strategy consulting, and secure, stable hosting environments for growing e-business enterprises.

Kleber is also President of Medical Assisted Services, Inc., a Florida-based medical company with several divisions, providing diagnostic testing services, pain-management solutions, and durable medical equipment to Physicians and healthcare professionals throughout the US.

Kleber is also a contributing technology reviewer for *Mac Design Magazine* and *Photoshop User*, and he has more than a decade of experience analyzing and implementing business computing infrastructures based on the Windows platform. Through his existing businesses, Kleber designs and develops real-world network and administrative solutions based on Microsoft technologies and the Windows OS architecture.

Kleber lives in the Tampa Bay area of Florida with his wife, Debbie, his son, Jarod, and his daughter, Jenna.

FOREWORD by Scott Kelby

As Editor for the Killer Tips series, I'm excited to not only bring you another Killer Tips book, but I'm particularly excited to introduce you to an author who is going to take you to a whole new level of speed, efficiency, productivity, and sheer un-adulterated out-and-out fun using Windows XP. (I just realized that when you put the words "sheer" and "unadulterated" together, it sounds kind of dirty, but it's not meant to be. That comes later.) But first, a little background on this book and why it's different from every other Windows book out there.

The idea for this type of book came to me one day when I was at the bookstore, browsing in the computer section, when I thought to myself, "Man, these authors must be making a ton of money!" No wait, that wasn't what I was thinking (it's close, mind you, but not exactly). Actually, I was standing there flipping though the different books on Adobe Photoshop (I'm a Photoshop guy at heart). Basically, what I would do is look for pages that had a tip on them. They're usually pretty easy to find, because these "rich book authors" usually separate their tips from the regular text of the book. Most of the time, they'll put a box around the tips, or add a tint behind them, maybe a Tip icon—something to make them stand out and get the readers' attention.

Anyway, that's what I would do—find a tip, read it, and then start flipping until I found another tip. The good news—the tips were usually pretty cool. You have to figure that if an author has some really slick trick, maybe a hidden keyboard shortcut or a cool workaround, they probably won't bury it in blocks of boring copy. No way! They'll find some way to get your attention (with those boxes, tints, a little icon, or simply the word "Tip!"). So, that's the cool news—if it said tip, it was usually worth checking out. The bad news—there were never enough tips. Sometimes they'd have five or six tips in a chapter, but other times, just one or two. But no matter how many they had, I always got to the last chapter and thought, "Man, I wish there had been more tips."

Standing right there in the bookstore, I thought to myself, "I wish there were a book with nothing but tips: hundreds of tips, cover-to-cover, and nothing else." Now *that's* a book I'd go crazy for. I kept looking and looking, but the book I wanted just wasn't available. That's when I got the idea to write one myself. The next day I called my editor to pitch him the idea. I told him it would be a book that would be wall-to-wall, nothing but cool tips, hidden shortcuts, and inside tricks designed to make Photoshop users faster, more productive, and best of all, to make using Photoshop even more fun. Well, he loved the idea. Okay, that's stretching it a bit. He *liked* the idea, but most importantly, he "green-lighted it" (that's Hollywood talk—I'm not quite sure what it means), and soon I had created my first all-tips book, *Photoshop 6 Killer Tips* (along with my co-author and good friend, *Photoshop User* magazine Creative Director Felix Nelson).

As it turned out, *Photoshop 6 Killer Tips* was an instant hit (fortunately for me and my chance-taking editor), and we followed it up with (are you ready for this?) *Photoshop 7 Killer Tips*, which was an even bigger hit. These books really struck a chord with readers, and I like to think it was because Felix and I were so deeply committed to creating something special—a book where every page included yet another tip that would make you nod your head, smile, and think "Ahhh, so that's how they do it." However, it pretty much came down to this: People just love cool tips. That's why now there are also *Dreamweaver MX Killer Tips* and *QuarkXPress 6 Killer Tips* books.

So how did we wind up here, with a Killer Tips book for an operating system? Well, there was an intermediate step: Last year I wrote *Mac OS X Killer Tips* for Macintosh users switching over to Apple's new UNIX-based operating system. It turned out to be such a big hit; it actually became "biggety-big" (a purely technical term only used during secret book-publishing rituals).

So creating a Windows XP Killer Tips book was a natural. The only problem is that I'm really a Photoshop guy and for this book to surpass the Mac book's "biggety-bigness," it would take a pretty special author. It would take a person who was an absolute Windows XP expert (with a giant über-brain), who has professional writing experience, a great sense of humor, and a casual, conversational writing style. This person would have to have a keen sense for uncovering those inside tips that the pros use to get twice the work done in half the time. They'd have to be one of those people who don't do anything "the hard way," and they'd have to know every timesaving shortcut, every workaround, and every speed tip to make something different, something special, and the only book of its kind in a very crowded Windows XP book market.

Here's the thing: I knew just the guy—Kleber Stephenson. I chose him for one simple reason: the similarity of his first name to my last name. Heck, it's almost the same name (Kleber Kelby. See what I mean?) That was enough for me. Okay, that's actually not the reason at all (just a lucky coincidence). I chose Kleber because he fit every criterion I had set for the ideal Killer Tips author. First, he totally "gets" the Killer Tips concept because just like me, he's a tip hound—a tip junkie (if you will). Second, I've always enjoyed his writing style, humor, the completeness of his research and attention to detail, and how he really immerses himself in a project. Third, like me he's a die-hard Tampa Bay Bucs fan. Fourth (and perhaps most important), he knows more Windows tips and has a better understanding of the Windows Operating System than anyone I know. Period. That's why, when we decided to do the book, I called him first, and honestly if he had decided to pass on the project, you wouldn't be reading this book now, because he was *so* the right person to do this book that I didn't have another person in mind as a backup plan. I wanted Kleber, and if I couldn't get him, I'd shelve the idea and move on to another project. That's how strongly I felt that he was the right person for the job, and I'm absolutely delighted that you're holding his book right now. Kleber has really captured the spirit and flavor of what a Killer Tips book is all about, and I can tell you this—you're gonna love it!

I can't wait for you to "get into it," so I'll step aside and let him take the wheel, because you're about to get faster, more efficient, and have more fun using Windows XP than you ever thought possible.

All my best,

Scott Kelby
Series Editor

TABLE OF CONTENTS

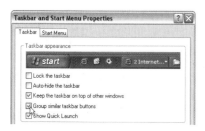

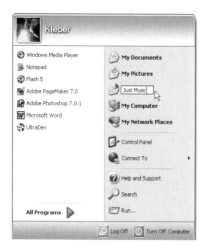

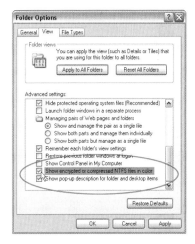

TABLE OF CONTENTS

CHAPTER 6 108
We Will Rock You
Rockin' Windows Tips

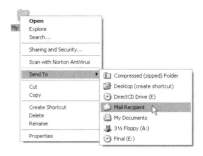

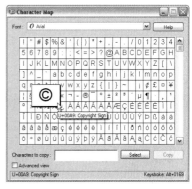

TABLE OF CONTENTS

It's a Small World
Explore Your World with Internet Explorer

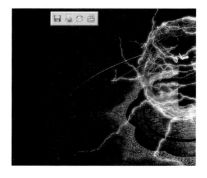

T A B L E O F CONTENTS

Chapter 10
It's a Wrap
Movie Making with Windows Movie Maker 2

TABLE OF CONTENTS

Feeling Fearless?
Windows XP Registry Hacks

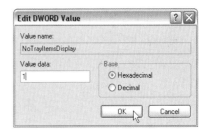

TELL US WHAT YOU THINK

As the reader of this book, you are the most important critic and commentator. We value your opinion and want to know what we're doing right, what we could do better, what areas you'd like to see us publish in, and any other words of wisdom you're willing to pass our way.

As the Executive Editor on this book, I welcome your comments. You can fax, email, or write me directly to let me know what you did or didn't like about this book—as well as what we can do to make our books stronger. When you write, please be sure to include this book's title, ISBN, and author, as well as your name and phone or fax number. I will carefully review your comments and share them with the author and editors who worked on the book.

Please note that I cannot help you with technical problems related to the topic of this book, and that due to the high volume of email I receive, I might not be able to reply to every message.

Fax: 317-428-3280

Email: steve.weiss@newriders.com

Mail: Steve Weiss

        Executive Editor

        New Riders Publishing

        800 E. 96th St., Suite 200

        Indianapolis, IN 46240 USA

Windows...
Wide Open

GET THE MOST OUT
OF WINDOWS XP

Ah, the beginning, the first chapter of my first book. And you're actually reading the chapter description for the first chapter of

Windows...Wide Open

get the most out of windows xp

my first book! That's just so cool! But you're probably already getting bored with this whole first-chapter-description thing and want to jump right into the tips. I can't really blame you (actually I can, but I won't). This book's loaded with great tips and I'm not just saying that because I wrote it. No, really, I'm not. Okay, I guess I am. But cut me a little slack, as this book was extremely tough to write. All right, it wasn't extremely tough. It wasn't like pulling-an-airplane-with-my-teeth tough, but it wasn't super-easy either. Anyway, this chapter's mostly about windows, folders, and toolbars, and is there anything more exciting than windows, folders and toolbars? Well just maybe having you read the chapter description for the first chapter of my first book. That's just so cool!

 ## TWO CLICKS ARE TOO MUCH

It just makes sense that if you can do the same thing in Windows with a single click of the mouse that you can do with two clicks, you'd take the shorter route, right? To take this one-click path, click Start, click My Computer, click Tools on the Menu Bar, and click Folder Options (Start>My Computer>Tools>Folder Options). Now click the General tab in the dialog box, choose Single-click to open an item (point to select), and then click OK. This makes everything in Windows exactly one click faster.

 ## THAT PICTURE SUITS ME

It's actually kind of cute that Windows requires you to associate your User Account with a picture—okay, not really. Since Microsoft didn't give you an easy way to turn off this feature, you might as well find a photo that suits you. To do this, click Start and then click the picture next to your name at the top of the Start menu. This opens the User Accounts window where you can select a new picture or browse your hard drive for something different (if rubber ducks and soccer balls aren't for you). After you've made your selection, click Change Picture and you're done.

MAY I SEE A MENU PLEASE?

By default, Windows lists many of the Start menu items, such as the Control Panel, as links. This means that when you click the item, a new window opens. You can, however, view these items as menus instead. For example, if you want to view the Control Panel as a menu, then right-click Start and click Properties on the Shortcut menu. Next, click the Start Menu tab in the dialog box and choose Customize Start Menu. Now, click on the Advanced tab. Under Start Menu Items, locate the Control Panel item, click Display as a Menu, and then click OK. Now, when you point to Control Panel, a menu will pop up listing its contents.

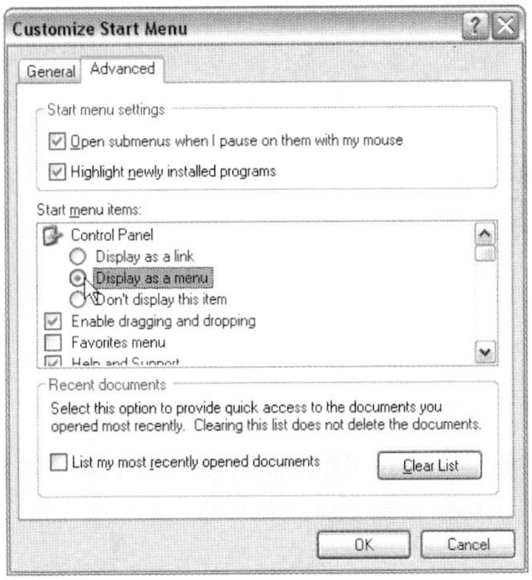

GIVE THE TRUE GIFT OF LOVE...SHARE YOUR COMPUTER

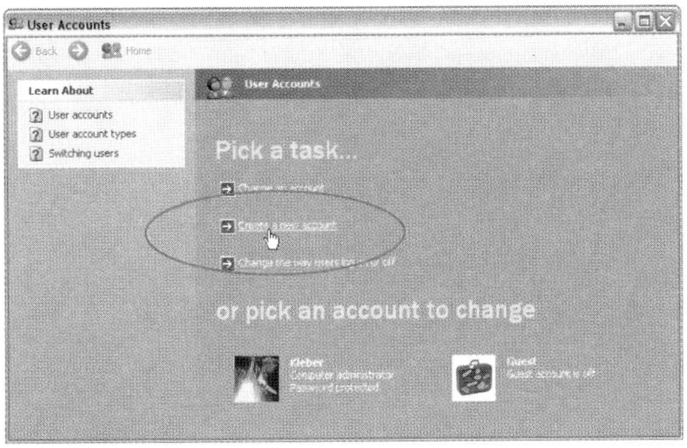

I know what you're going to say—sharing your computer is about as much fun as sharing your toothbrush. But since you're gonna have to do it, why not avoid some of the pain and create User Accounts? There are tons of advantages to this, the most obvious being that users get to personalize Windows to their own tastes, and you get to protect your important documents. So when you're ready, click Start and open the Control Panel. Next, click the User Accounts icon, click Create a New Account, and follow the setup instructions. You'll be asked to provide a name for the new user and to pick the account type. After you've answered these questions, click Create Account.

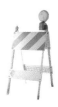

 NOT SURE ABOUT A FILE? JUST DROP IT

UltraDev

Hmm...File

Microsoft
Word

Adobe
Photosh...

Every once in a while you'll get an odd file. You just can't tell what kind of file it is and there's no program associated with it. Here's a way to try to find a program that can open it: Drag-and-drop the file onto different programs' icons. If the program can open the file, then the App will launch to display the file. If the program can't open the file, then the "unavailable" cursor pops up.

 ANOTHER WAY TO MAXIMIZE AND RESTORE WINDOWS

Instead of struggling to click the Maximize or Restore buttons on a window's Title Bar—you know, the square buttons about the size of a mini Chiclet—try this. Double-click the window's Title Bar to maximize the window. To restore the window, double-click the Title Bar again.

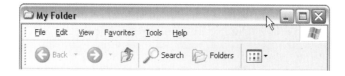

MINIMIZE USING THE TASKBAR

Next time you're minimizing a window, use the Taskbar. Instead of going for the Chiclets on the Title Bar, try clicking the window's Taskbar button, which will minimize the window. Click the Taskbar button again to restore the window. Try doing this really fast for a nice strobe effect!

 ## CLOSE USING THE TASKBAR

Sticking with this whole Chiclets thing—there's also a way to avoid them when closing a window. Right-click the window's Taskbar button and click Close on the Shortcut menu.

 DON'T JUST MAXIMIZE YOUR WINDOWS—GO FULL SCREEN

When you need a really big window, don't just maximize it: Go full screen! To view a window full screen, hold down the Ctrl key and double-click the window's Title Bar—or when the window's active, press the F11 key at the top of your keyboard—to get the biggest window possible.

 MANUALLY RESIZE A WINDOW

Scroll your mouse to any edge of a window's four sides until you see the vertical or horizontal resize cursors. The arrows tell you which way you can drag the window's border. When the cursor pops up, click-and-hold with your mouse, and drag to resize the window. If you want to resize two sides at once, you can grab any of the four corners of a window the same way and drag to make your window instantly smaller or larger.

RESIZE A MAXIMIZED WINDOW

To resize a maximized window, scroll your mouse over the middle button (it looks like two stacked boxes) located top-right on the window's Title Bar button (see image). This is the Restore Down button. If you hold your mouse over the button for a moment, a description of the button will pop up. Click the Restore Down button and this decreases the size of your window without minimizing it. Now, you can adjust the window to any size you like.

 CHANGE WHICH APP OPENS A FILE

You use Windows Media Player to open your music files (MP3s, WAVs, etc.), and you like it that way. Well, you've just downloaded and installed a new music player and suddenly your MP3s are opening in your newly installed player, not in the Windows Media Player. What's up with that? Wait, don't start uninstalling software; there's an easier way to get your music files back. Right-click the icon of any MP3 file and click Properties on the Shortcut menu. Then, click the General tab in the dialog box and click Change. On the Open With dialog box, scroll the Recommended Programs, click Windows Media Player, and click OK. Now, click OK on the General tab. Whew, that's better! Use this same technique to associate programs with any file type.

YOU CAN MAKE IT SMALLER IF YOU SQUEEZE IT

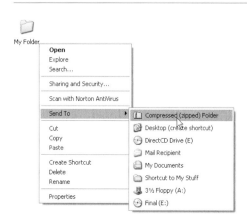

Windows XP makes it easier than ever to compress or zip files. This is especially handy when you want to e-mail a folder containing several files (compressing a file can make it considerably smaller, and thus faster to e-mail) or to protect and store data. To compress a file or folder, right-click the file you want to compress, point to Send To and click Compressed (Zipped) Folder on the Shortcut menu. Windows will immediately create a new compressed folder in the same location as the source file. You'll be able to identify the new compressed folder by a little zipper on the folder's icon.

MAKE ROOM! COMPRESS FOLDERS AND DIRECTORIES

If you have folders or directories that contain many large files, compress them. Not only does this save a ton of space, but you can also work with compressed folders the same way as any other folder. Right-click your folder and click Properties on the Shortcut menu. Next, click the General tab in the dialog box, then click Advanced Attributes. Check Compress Contents to Save Disk Space, then click OK.

CHANGE YOUR VIEWS

Windows XP offers new and improved ways to view files, and it's easy to find the view that works best for you. From an open window, click Views on the Standard Buttons Toolbar. You'll have several views available to you. Click each view to see how it affects your files. You can set views differently for folders, so play around with them until you find the best view for your folder. For instance, you'd probably want to view a folder containing photos differently than you would a folder containing documents.

 ## NICE VIEW! I THINK I'LL SAVE IT

Okay, you've found the perfect folder view. The view just seems to work for everything. Wouldn't it be nice if you were able to apply that view to all your folders with just a click of the mouse? Well, you can't. It's impossible (just kidding).

To give all your folders the same view, open the folder with the view that you want to apply to them and, on the folder's Menu Bar, click Tools>Folder Options. Next, click the View tab in the dialog box and choose Apply to All Folders. You'll be asked to confirm your request. Click Yes, and now all the folders on your computer will have the same view.

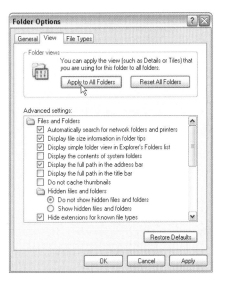

 WANT MORE TOOLBAR BUTTONS? WHO CAN BLAME YOU?

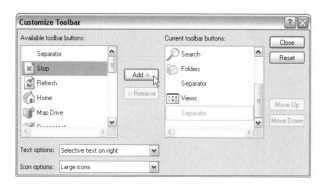

Hey, who doesn't want more buttons? They're cute. Get it, cute as buttons (sorry, that was bad!). Here's how you can quickly customize your Toolbar with all kinds of useful and cute buttons (I just can't leave it alone). To check out all of the Toolbar buttons available to you, right-click the Standard Buttons Toolbar and click Customize on the Shortcut menu.

Simply scroll the Available Toolbar buttons on the left side of the dialog box. When you find a button that you want to add, click to highlight it, and then click Add (in the center of the dialog box). You'll see that the button now appears in the Current Toolbar Buttons on the right of the window. When you're finished, click Close.

 TOOLBARS GETTING CROWDED? SHRINK THE ICONS

What are you going to do now that you have every single available button on your Toolbar? The answer is: Shrink 'em. Right-click the Standard Buttons Toolbar and click Customize on the Shortcut menu. Next, select Small Icons from the Icon options drop-down menu (see image) and click Close. Look at all that room! I think I need more buttons!

ORGANIZE ICONS ON YOUR TOOLBAR

This is really kind of clunky. (Is clunky a word?) Anyway, if you want to change the order of your Toolbar buttons, right-click the Standard Buttons Toolbar and click Customize on the Shortcut menu. On the right of the dialog box, click in the Current Toolbar Buttons window to highlight the button that you want to move. Now, use the Move Up and Move Down but-

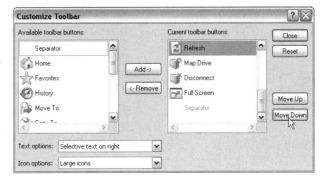

tons (on the right) to change the order of the buttons, and click Close. Wouldn't it be nice if you could just grab the Toolbar buttons with your mouse and drag them where you want? (Hmmmm...In case anyone from Microsoft is reading this book: Wouldn't it be nice if you could just grab the Toolbar buttons with your mouse and drag them where you want?)

 ## KEEP 'EM SEPARATED

You can also organize your buttons into groups—sort of—by putting a separator between similar buttons to help make them a little easier to locate. Right-click the Standard Buttons Toolbar and click Customize on the Shortcut menu. Scroll the Available Toolbar buttons (on the left side) until you see a button named—you guessed it—Separator. Click to highlight it and then click Add. Now move the Separator up or down to position it and click Close.

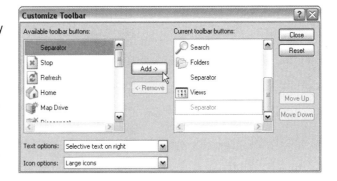

 WHAT ARE THOSE LITTLE BLACK ARROWS ON MY TOOLBAR?

When your window's Toolbar is too short to display all your Toolbar buttons, you'll see two little black arrows to the right of the Toolbar. These arrows tell you that you have additional buttons on the Toolbar. Clicking the arrows will display a menu of the unseen buttons. You can also stretch your window, making the Toolbar larger until you no longer see the arrows.

 TOOLBARS A MESS? GET BACK YOUR DEFAULTS

Okay, you've been playing with your Toolbars for hours when you realize that the only thing you've accomplished is a big mess. There's a way to get you quickly back to normal. Right-click the Standard Buttons Toolbar and click Customize Toolbar on the Shortcut menu. Under Close, to the right, you'll find the Reset button. Click Reset and the Standard Buttons Toolbar goes back to its default setting.

FINALLY! TOOLBARS THE WAY YOU LIKE THEM

It's inevitable. You finally get your Toolbars set up just the way you like them when suddenly your four-year-old comes flying by, knocks your arm and BAM! Toolbars all over the place. When this happens, there's a way to keep from having to start over—lock 'em.

When you have your Toolbars set up, right-click any Toolbar, and click Lock the Toolbars on the Shortcut menu. Now, not even a nuclear blast will move them. Of course, if you ever do want to move them again, just right-click any Toolbar and deselect Lock the Toolbars on the Shortcut menu.

 ## LINKS...THE ULTIMATE TOOLBAR

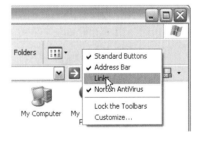

You know what would make a great Toolbar? One where you could put your favorite Apps and documents so that you could open them from any window at any time. Guess what? You can and here's how: Click Start, then My Computer. Now right-click the Standard Buttons Toolbar and then click Links on the Shortcut menu. You now have the Links Toolbar on your windows (the same Links Toolbar that's in Internet Explorer). *Note:* Make sure that Lock the Toolbars is not checked. Click on it to deselect it if it is.

The really cool thing about the Links Toolbar is that it's completely customizable—try this: Navigate to your favorite App and drag-and-drop its icon to the Links Toolbar. You just created a shortcut. Do this again and again for as many Apps as you want to appear on the Toolbar.

 ADD NEW FOLDERS TO THE LINKS TOOLBAR

 To keep your shortcuts better organized on the Links Toolbar, you can create folders to hold them. From an open window's Menu Bar, click File, point to New, and then click Folder to create a new folder in the window. Rename the folder to whatever you like. Next, while holding down the Ctrl key, drag-and-drop the folder onto the Links Toolbar. Instead of creating a shortcut to the new folder, you just created a copy of the folder on the Toolbar. Delete the new folder from the window (not the Links Toolbar), as you don't need it anymore. Now you can start dragging-and-dropping shortcuts to the folder instead of directly onto the Toolbar.

 REARRANGE THE LINKS TOOLBAR ICONS

 After you have your folders and shortcuts on the Links Toolbar, you can easily rearrange them in any order you want. Just click-and-hold, then drag-and-drop them onto the Toolbar in any order. (If only the Standard Buttons Toolbar was this friendly.)

THEY'RE ICONS; YOU CAN CHANGE 'EM

If you want to change your Links Toolbar folders or shortcuts to different icons, go right ahead. Just like any other folder or shortcut, you can change them to whatever you like. Here's how: Right-click the folder or shortcut on the Links Toolbar and click Properties on the Shortcut menu. If it's a shortcut's icon you're changing, click the Shortcut tab in the dialog box, then click Change Icon. Select a new icon then click OK. If you're changing a folder's icon, click the Customize tab, click the Change Icon button, then select a new icon, and click OK.

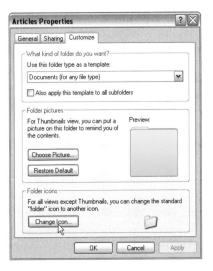

REMOVING THE LINKS TOOLBAR ICONS

If you want to remove a folder or shortcut from the Links Toolbar, click-and-hold, then drag it to the Recycle bin. You can also right-click the shortcut and click Delete on the Shortcut menu.

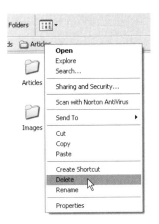

ANTI-SCROLL TIP—RIGHT-MOUSE-CLICK

Right-clicking the Scroll Bar in Windows will display a Shortcut menu with several scroll options. Choose Scroll Here to scroll automatically to where you right-clicked the window's Scroll Bar.

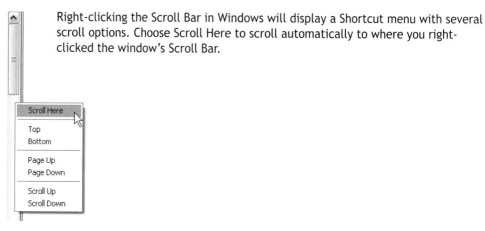 ANTI-SCROLL TIP—USE THE KEYBOARD

The next time you're scrolling away inside Windows, try using your keyboard instead. The Page Up and Page Down keys do exactly that—move the window's page up or down. Use the Home key to jump back to the top of a window, and the End key to zip to the bottom.

WHEEL MOUSE SCROLL TIP—ADJUST THE WHEEL

If you own a wheel mouse, then you can control how many lines your mouse will scroll when you turn the wheel. Click Start and open the Control Panel. Next, click the Printer and Other Hardware icon then the Mouse icon. (*Note*: This is in Category view, not Classic view.) Click the Wheel tab in the dialog box, change the number of lines your mouse will scroll with each turn of the wheel, and then click OK.

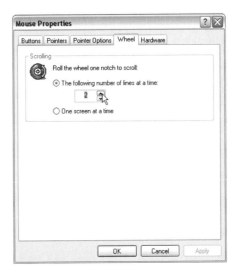

SERIOUS FOLDER POWER

Did you know that you can customize folders to suit their contents? You can. Right-click the folder and click Properties on the Shortcut menu. Next, click the Customize tab in the dialog box and locate the text, What Kind of Folder Do You Want? Now from the drop-down menu, select the type of folder: Pictures, Photo Album, Videos, and more. Different folder types will provide different common tasks in a window's Task Panel.

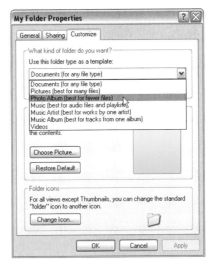

 APPLYING FOLDER TEMPLATES

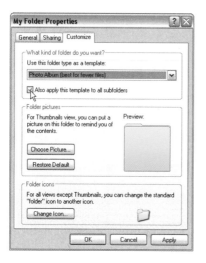

If you've customized a folder, and its subfolders pretty much contain the same types of files, then you should apply a folder template to the parent folder. This will apply your Preferences to each subfolder—perfect for categorizing digital photos. Here's what you do: Right-click the parent folder and click Properties on the Shortcut menu. Next, click the Customize tab in the dialog box and check the box below that reads Also Apply This Template to All Subfolders, then click OK.

 THAT'S BETTER THAN AN ICON

You can customize folders to make them a little more personal and easier to identify by putting a photo on the cover. First, make certain you're using Thumbnails or Filmstrip view, as you can only view pictures on your folders when you're in these views (on the Toolbar, then View>Filmstrip or Thumbnails). Right-click your folder and click Properties on the Shortcut menu. Next, click the Customize tab and click the Choose Picture button. Browse your hard drive for the photo that you want to use for your cover then click Apply.

WHAT ARE THOSE LITTLE BLACK ARROWS ON MY TASK PANES?

You can close or expand a common Task Pane using the two little black arrows located at the top right of each pane (see image). This comes in handy when viewing a file's details.

 ## REMOVE THE TASK PANEL

If you find that Windows' common Task Panel takes up more room than it provides help, you can turn it off. Click Start then My Computer. On the Menu Bar, click Tools, then Folder Options. Next, click the General tab in the dialog box, click Use Windows Classic Folders, and then click OK.

 USE FILMSTRIP VIEW TO BROWSE PICTURES

Whenever a folder contains picture files (JPEGs, GIFs, BMPs...), a Filmstrip view is available to you. Use this view to browse your pictures; it's way cool! You'll get a large preview of the image that you can adjust (make larger or smaller) by changing the size of the window.

 THE NOT-SO-OBVIOUS POWER OF FILMSTRIP VIEW

Now you know that Filmstrip view is great for viewing photos, but you can also do some other pretty cool things using this view. For example, you can rotate your picture, using the rotate icons directly below the preview—and this feature actually rotates the picture, not just the preview. You can also make any picture your Desktop background: Just right-click the picture and click Set as Desktop Background on the Shortcut menu.

OPEN FOLDERS IN DIFFERENT WINDOWS

By default, Windows XP opens folders in the same window, which is good because I really dislike new windows popping up all over my Desktop (I'm kind of a neat freak). If you're not like me, however, you can make folders open in different windows. Click Start>My Computer>Tools>Folder Options. Next, click the General tab in the dialog box, click Open Each Folder in Its Own Window, and then click OK.

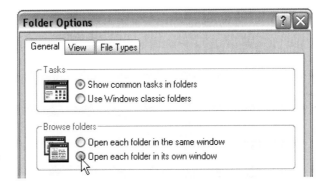

HMMM...IT NEEDS ITS OWN WINDOW

Here's the dilemma: Windows views folders in the same window but you need a particular folder to open in its own window. Here's how to do it. From within an open window, highlight the folder that you want to open in its own window. Hold the Ctrl key and then press Enter. Your folder will open in its own window. Problem solved! This tip also works for opening multiple selected folders in their own windows.

 INSTANTLY VIEW A FILE'S DETAILS

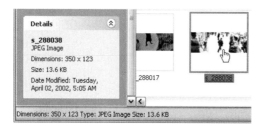

A quick way to get a file's details, such as when it was created, date it was last modified, and size, is to use the Details Pane on the Tasks Panel. Click the file once or move over it with your mouse (scroll) to highlight it. When the file is highlighted, you can view its details in the Details Task Pane.

 DON'T LIKE TOOLBARS? DON'T USE 'EM

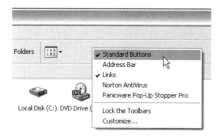

There are some of you (we won't name names, but we will name groups—DOS User group, Anywhere, USA), who actually don't feel a need to use Toolbars. Personally, I'm okay with that, but my wife...she'll let you have it. If you're not afraid of my wife, here's how to do it: Open My Computer from the Desktop, right-click the Standard Buttons Toolbar, and click each Toolbar on the Shortcut menu to uncheck it until your Toolbars are no more. Scary isn't it?

BROWSE THE WEB FROM ANY WINDOW

Windows XP is the most Web-integrated Operating System ever. And, nowhere is that more evident than the window right there in front of you. Just add an Address Toolbar and you can navigate the Web from  any open window on your Desktop. Open My Computer from the Desktop, right-click the Standard Buttons Toolbar, and click Address Bar on the Shortcut menu. Now just type in a URL or choose a site from Favorites and your window turns into a browser. Want to go back to your folder's window? Hit the Back button on the Toolbar.

 FIND FILES USING THE ADDRESS BAR

Of course you use the Address Bar to visit Web sites, but you can also use it to help locate files on your hard drive. Click the Down arrow on the Address Bar to view your hard drive. Click on a drive or directory to select it. Your selection will appear in the folder's window. Now you can browse the folders or drives until you locate your file(s).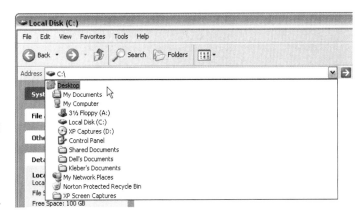

 POP-UP TASKBAR BUTTONS

 Press-and-hold the Alt key and then press the Tab key to display a pop-up dialog box that shows icons of your Taskbar items. Hit the Tab key again to move to the next icon and so on. After you've highlighted the item that you want, let go of the Alt key, and that window jumps to the foreground on your Desktop.

 VIEW STATUS BAR ON WINDOWS

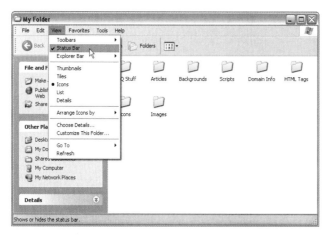 Another great way to view a file's details is by placing the Status Bar on your windows. Often the Details Pane is impossible to see because it's buried at the bottom of the Tasks Panel. But a quick glance at the Status Bar will tell you what you want to know. To enable the Status Bar on your windows, open My Computer from your Desktop, click View on the Menu Bar, and then click Status Bar.

SCREEN-SAVER SAFE

If you're the kind of person who's really freaky about your privacy, or you're working on top-secret government stuff (or maybe just doodling not-so-kind pictures of the boss in Paint), then it might be a good idea to password-protect your computer when it returns from a screen saver. (You never know, your boss might stop by when you're on a coffee break and accidentally bump your mouse.) Here's how to do it. Right-click your Desktop and click Properties on the Shortcut menu. Click the Screen Saver tab, then click On Resume, Password Protect to activate it. Click OK.

 ## CONTROL THE CONTROL PANEL

The new-look Control Panel takes some getting used to (the old Control Panel worked so well). If you really miss the old Control Panel, you can get it back. Click Start and open My Control Panel. In the top Task Pane (labeled Control Panel), click the Switch to Classic View link and there it is. Ah, much better!

 SIDE-BY-SIDE

You can display any two windows side-by-side on the Desktop by first clicking a window's button on the Taskbar. Next, press-and-hold the Ctrl key and right-click the second window that you want to open, then click Tile Vertically on the Shortcut menu. This works great when you want to view Word or Internet Explorer windows at the same time.

Have it
Your Way

CUSTOMIZE WINDOWS XP

This is my favorite chapter. It's probably going to be yours too. XP is a fantastic operating system that's only made better

Have It Your Way

customize windows xp

by how customizable it is. You really can have it your way! It's too bad I can't have everything in life my way. That'd be great! I'd make digital cameras the size of TVs so my family and friends wouldn't have to jockey for position to stare at a screen the size of a Cheez-It® just to see my son's T-ball pictures. And every elementary-school kid would get those skinny crayons. I grew up using the fat ones and still to this day can't color inside the lines. I'd send every flight attendant to a Tony Robbins "The Customer is My Friend and I Won't Be Rude Because They Ask Me to Do My Job" seminar. The Bucs (Tampa Bay Buccaneers©) would win the Super Bowl every year! Man, I love the Bucs! And, oh yeah, I'd allow school prayer. Yep, it sure would be great to have it my way! At least we can have Windows our way.

 GROUND CONTROL...WE HAVE ICONS

Okay, I honestly believe that astronauts on the Space Station can see my Start menu icons— they're that big. Let's change them to a size that doesn't give you vertigo every time you click Start.

Right-click Start and select Properties on the Shortcut menu. Next, click the Start Menu tab in the dialog box, and choose Customize Start menu. Now click the General tab, click Small Icons, then click OK.

 IT'S A-TO-Z FOR THE ALL PROGRAMS MENU

Being an A-to-Z kind of guy, I understand the alphabetical order, and it makes things easier to find. Apparently the All Programs menu doesn't. But here's a way to teach your All Programs menu the ABCs. Click Start and point to All Programs. Right-click the Programs menu anywhere and choose Sort by Name on the Shortcut menu. That's much better!

DON'T LIKE THE NEW START MENU? CHANGE IT BACK

If Windows XP's new Start menu just isn't doing it for you, then switch it back to Windows Classic Start menu. Right-click Start and choose Properties on the Shortcut menu. Next, click the Start Menu tab in the dialog box and click the Classic Start Menu. Click OK.

MORE PROGRAMS ON THE START MENU

By default, the Start menu will show your seven most frequently used programs, which is really convenient. In fact, it's so convenient I think I'd like to see—I don't know—how about 30 of my most frequently used programs.

Right-click Start and click Properties on the Shortcut menu. Next, click the Start Menu tab in the dialog box and click Customize. Now, just crank up the number (up to 30) of the frequently used programs that you'd like to see on the Start menu, then click OK.

 "PIN" PROGRAMS TO THE START MENU

Want to add your favorite
programs to the Start Menu?
Click Start and point to All
Programs. Locate a favorite
program, right-click the
program's icon, and select
Pin to Start Menu on the
Shortcut menu. That's it.
You can also pin an App by
dragging-and-dropping its

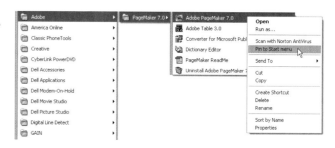

icon from the All Programs menu on the Start menu. The program is now "pinned" to your
Start menu. To remove it, right-click the program icon on the Start menu then click Unpin
from Start Menu on the Shortcut menu.

 SCROLL YOUR PROGRAMS INSTEAD

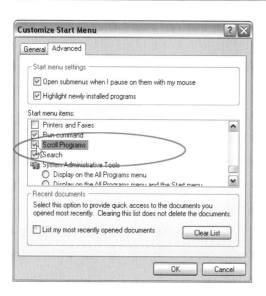

There's something annoying about opening
the All Programs menu. Maybe it's the
way that it covers my entire Desktop. It's
almost scary the way it jumps out at you.
I prefer to scroll my programs all in one
nice, compact menu. If you do too, here's
how: Right-click Start and choose Properties on the Shortcut menu. Next, click
the Start Menu tab in the dialog box, then
click the Customize button to the right of
Start menu. Now, click the Advanced tab
and scroll the items in Start Menu Items
until you see Scroll Programs. Check this
option and then click OK.

MY, MY, MY...WE GET IT

Why does Windows name all your personal folders in the Start menu with "My" as the first word? I know it's mine. "My" just seems a little rhetorical on every folder. Did you know that you can rename the "My" folders? Yes, you can! Click Start and point to any "My" folder, right-click its name, and click Rename on the Shortcut menu. Now, type in a new name for your folder—preferably something without "My" in the title.

 ## THE INTERNET ON YOUR TASKBAR

Have you ever wanted to launch a Web page from your Taskbar? Of course you have, and here's how: Right-click the Taskbar, point to Toolbars and click Address on the Shortcut menu. Now an Internet Address Bar appears on your Taskbar. Simply type in a URL, then click Go or press Enter on your keyboard to open the page in Internet Explorer.

 TASKBAR WEB PAGES

Maybe having the Address Bar on your Taskbar isn't good enough for you? You've got to actually put a Web page on your Taskbar. Okay, right-click the Taskbar, point to Toolbars, and click New Toolbar on the Shortcut menu. In the Folder text box, type the Web page's complete URL (include http://), then click OK.

 LAUNCH APPS FROM THE ADDRESS BAR

What if you could launch an App from the Address Bar? Wouldn't that be cool? So try this: Open the Address Toolbar by right-clicking the Taskbar, point to Toolbars, and choose Address on the Shortcut menu. In the Address Bar type "notepad" (without the quotes), then click Go. You just launched Notepad from your Address Bar.

FAVORITES ALL THE TIME

Put Favorites on the Taskbar and you'll never have to launch Internet Explorer again to find a favorite site. Are you ready? Right-click the Taskbar, point to Toolbars, and click New Toolbar on the Shortcut menu. Use the dialog box to navigate to Favorites, usually located at C:\Documents and Settings\your user name\Favorites, and click the folder to select it. Click OK and you're done. Now you have the Favorites menu on the Taskbar. This also works for adding any folder to the Taskbar.

FLOATING TOOLBARS? COOL!

The previous tip showed you how to put a folder on your Taskbar, which is cool; but it gets really wild when you start yankin' them off and floatin' them on your Desktop. To float your Toolbars, grab a Toolbar with your mouse and simply drag it onto your Desktop and let go. Floating Toolbars—Cool! You can also change the size of these windows or dock them on an edge of your Desktop.

 QUICK, LAUNCH IT!

As far as Toolbars go, there's none more useful than the Quick Launch Toolbar. Quick Launch gives fast access to Internet Explorer and Outlook Express and it holds the Show Desktop icon. To open your Quick Launch Toolbar, right-click the Taskbar, point to Toolbars, and choose Quick Launch on the Shortcut menu. The Quick Launch Toolbar appears directly to the right of Start.

 QUICK LAUNCH YOUR FAVORITE APPS

There's no need to clutter your Desktop with shortcuts to your favorite programs. Quick Launch is the perfect place to hold them. Simply, drag-and-drop your shortcuts to the Quick Launch Toolbar. Now, your favorite Apps are just one click away, always visible, and not cluttering up the Desktop.

  MOVING QUICK LAUNCH ICONS

It's easy to re-order your icons after they're on the
Quick Launch Toolbar. Just grab them with your mouse
and move them left or right to drop them in any order
you want.

  ONE-CLICK SEARCH

Search is also a perfect place for the Quick
Launch Toolbar. I use it all the time and the
more convenient it is to get to, the better.
To add Search to your Toolbar, click Start
then click-and-hold Search, and drag-and-
drop it onto the Quick Launch Toolbar.

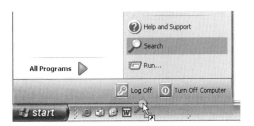

 TASKBAR...ON THE MOVE

  The Taskbar is undoubtedly the most important tool in Windows. It's where everything happens. You'd think that something so important couldn't be fooled with, wouldn't you? Well, fool away my friend. Click-and-hold the Taskbar with your mouse and you can drag it all over the place. Dock the Taskbar on any side of the Desktop; top, left, right, it doesn't matter.

 STRETCH! AH, THAT'S BETTER

Sometimes your Taskbar gets a little tight and cramped for room. When this happens, give it a stretch. Scroll your mouse over the top edge of the Taskbar until you see the vertical resize cursor. Click-and-hold and drag it up. Isn't that better?

PEEK-A-BOO WITH THE TASKBAR

You don't have to always look at the Taskbar; you can hide it when you're not using
it. Right-click Start and click Properties on
the Shortcut menu. Next, click the Taskbar
tab in the dialog box, check Auto-Hide the
Taskbar, and then click OK. When you want
the Taskbar to reappear, just move your
cursor to the bottom of the Desktop and it
pops back up.

 HIDE THE TASKBAR MANUALLY

If for any reason you need to hide the Taskbar,
but don't necessarily want to use auto-hide, you
can hide it manually. Scroll your mouse over the

top edge of the Taskbar until you see the vertical resize cursor. Click-and-hold and drag it
down out of view. To get it back, move your cursor to the bottom of the Desktop, and when
it again changes to the vertical resize cursor, click-and-drag the Taskbar back into view.

 A DESKTOP YOU CAN ALWAYS SEE

Placing your Desktop on the Taskbar gives you a quick way to access it. You'll no longer have to minimize windows to get to your Desktop folders and icons. To add the Desktop to your Taskbar, right-click the Taskbar, point to Toolbars, and click Desktop on the Short-cut menu. Your Desktop now appears as a pop-up menu on the Taskbar.

 MAKE SOME ROOM: STACK 'EM

Are too many Toolbars making the Taskbar more of a task than a bar (just couldn't resist)? Then, stack them. To do this, move your cursor to the Toolbars you want to move, scroll over the Toolbar separator on the left of the Toolbar until you see the horizontal move cursor, and then simply drag the Toolbars beneath one another to stack them in any order you want.

 ## HUDDLE UP, GROUP YOUR BUTTONS

Know how every time you open a new window, a new Taskbar button appears? Of course you do. Isn't it kind of a pain digging through these buttons trying to find a particular window? Sure it is. Well, Windows XP helps to solve this problem. You can now group similar buttons.

Right-click Start and click Properties on the Shortcut menu. Next, click the Taskbar tab in the dialog box, check Group similar Taskbar buttons, and then click OK. Now when several documents of the same type are open, they'll group together in a menu.

 ## SPEED TIP: CLOSE A GROUP AT ONCE

Grouped buttons also allow you to handle the group as you would a single button. Right-click the group's button to view its Shortcut menu. From its Shortcut menu, you can choose from several actions, including closing them all at once.

 IF I'M NOT USING 'EM, I DON'T WANT TO SEE 'EM

For whatever reason, software manufactur-ers want to put their icon in the notifica-tion area of your Taskbar. Unfortunately, there's not an awful lot you can do about it, but...there is a way where you won't have to look at them.

Right-click Start and click Properties on the Shortcut menu. Next, click the Taskbar tab in the dialog box, check Hide Inactive Icons, and then click OK. This will hide the icons when they aren't being used by Windows—which means you'll never see most of them again.

 YOU'VE BEEN NOTIFIED...YOU'VE GOT TO GO

If you don't ever want to see icons in your noti-fication area, regardless whether or not they're in use, here's how: Right-click Start and click Properties on the Shortcut menu. Next, click the Taskbar tab in the dialog box then click Custom-ize. Scroll the items listed and click its Behavior to the right to change its status. When you're through, click OK.

PUMP UP THE VOLUME

Turn up (or down) the volume on your computer without ever touching your speaker's volume controls. I know this isn't an earth-shattering tip, but I bet for some people this tip makes buying this book completely worthwhile (or completely worthless, I'm not sure which?). Click Start, open the Control Panel, then click the Sounds, Speech, and Audio Devices icon. Next, click the Sounds and Audio Devices icon, check Place Volume Icon in the Taskbar, and then click OK. Now, you can adjust your computer's volume right from the Taskbar.

 DO YOU NEED THE TIME?

If you're desperately in need of more Taskbar space and you have absolutely no need to know the time, then you can remove the clock and free up at least another whopping five-eighths of an inch. Right-click Start and click Properties on the Shortcut menu. Next, click the Taskbar tab in the dialog box, uncheck Show the Clock, and click OK.

And, how is it that you don't need a clock anyway? Never mind, I don't want to know. It's none of my business.

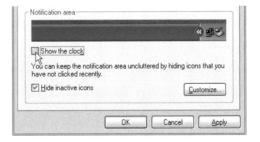

WORK OUT OF YOUR BRIEFCASE

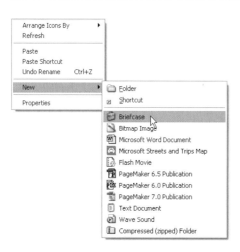

I travel a lot and work out of Windows Brief-cases all the time. They're great for syn-chronizing files between my laptop and other computers, but Windows doesn't make it very easy to create them. At least you might think that, if you went searching for them. Actually they're just one click away from anywhere you'd want to create one. Right-click your Desktop (or in any folder), point to New, and click Briefcase on the Shortcut menu. It's so obvious, I bet you missed it.

IT'S TIME FOR A CHANGE

There's something about sitting and staring at the same Desktop background day in and day out that just sucks time from me. Honestly, I easily forget the day of the week after a couple hours in front of my computer. Don't let this happen to you (it's too late for me). Change your Desktop background occasionally.

Right-click the Desktop and click Properties on the Shortcut menu. Next, click the Desk-top tab in the dialog box and scroll for a new background or click Browse to search your hard drive. You can preview your selections in the Desktop preview above. Click to highlight your new background then click OK.

I PREFER SOLIDS

Ok, you're a meat-and-potatoes kind of person and background pictures make you think too much. You stress over trying to find a picture that identifies you—who you are as a person. You can almost feel the anxiety, can't you? Don't put yourself through it....just pick a color for your background. Colors are easy.

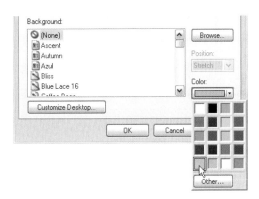

Right-click the Desktop and click Properties on the Shortcut menu. Next, click the Desktop tab in the dialog box and click None for your Background. Now pick a color from the Color Picker button to the right and click OK. Are you feeling better yet?

 IT'S NOT A THEME PARK, BUT IT'S CLOSE

You can easily change the entire look of your Desktop in Windows—backgrounds, pointers, colors, icons, you name it—which is great because the developers at Microsoft and I definitely don't have the same tastes.

Right-click the Desktop and click Properties on the Shortcut menu. Next, click the Themes tab in the dialog box and click the Theme Bar's Down arrow. Scroll for a new Desktop theme and when you've found that perfect one, click OK.

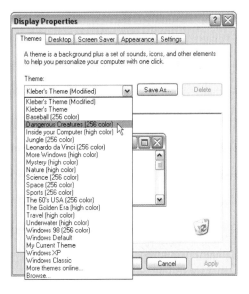

 CREATE CUSTOM THEMES

What's the point in having a theme for your personal computer if you can't make it personal? There's no point, and Microsoft knew this. So, here's how to customize a personal theme. First, use the previous tip to select a Theme. While you're still in the Display Properties dialog box, click the Desktop, Screen Saver, and Appearance tabs to make new choices for these items. Click Apply each time you make a change. OK will close the dialog box. When you're finished, go back to the Themes tab, click Save As, give your new theme a name, and then click Save. You've just made a custom theme.

 APPEARING LIVE ON YOUR DESKTOP...YOUR FAVORITE WEB PAGE

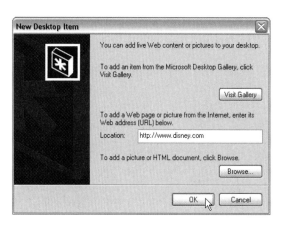

That's right! Your favorite Web page, live appearing on your Desktop, and in its own window! You can make its window bigger, smaller, move it around, or anything—just like any window— here's how: Right-click the Desktop and click Properties on the Shortcut menu. Next, click the Desktop tab in the dialog box and choose Customize Desktop. Click the Web tab in the dialog box then New. Now, just type your favorite URL in the Location text box and click OK.

A REFRESHING DESKTOP

Now that you've created a live Desktop Web page, you'll want to keep it fresh—as in refreshed. To do this manually, right-click the Desktop and click Properties on the Shortcut menu. Next, click the Desktop tab in the dialog box then click Customize Desktop. Click the Web tab in the dialog box, select the Web page you want to refresh, and click Synchronize.

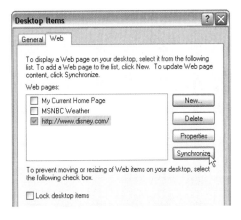

You can also schedule the Web page to refresh automatically. With the Web page selected, click Properties then click the Schedule tab. Click Using the Following Schedule(s). Choose Add to create a time and click OK.

 ADD COOL WEB STUFF TO YOUR DESKTOP

Is it snowing outside? Probably not for me, as I live in Florida. But if I had the weather on my Desktop, I'd know the answer without having to look outside. Well, just so I don't have to risk seeing that white stuff, I think I'll go ahead and put the weather on my Desktop. You can, too.

Right-click the Desktop and click Properties on the Shortcut menu. Next, click the Desktop tab in the dialog box and click Customize Desktop. Click the Web tab in the dialog box and click New. Click Visit Gallery, which will launch your browser and take you to Microsoft's Desktop Gallery. Here you can select all kinds of cool live Web items to place on your Desktop—including the weather. Find the item you want and click Add to Active Desktop.

 ANIMATE YOUR DESKTOP

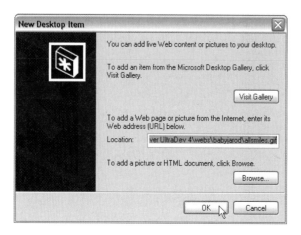

Because your Windows Desktop can display all kinds of Web stuff, it only makes sense that you can put Web animations (as in animated GIFs) on it as well. So, if you're in the mood to have bouncing balls and spinning planets doin' their thing all over your Desktop, just follow these steps: Right-click the Desktop and click Properties on the Shortcut menu. Next, click the Desktop tab in the dialog box then choose Customize Desktop. Click the Web tab in the dialog box and then New. Now, click Browse to locate any animated GIF or even an HTML document you'd like to place on your Desktop. After you've selected your file, click OK. Entertainment has never been so cheap.

 LOCK WEB ITEMS

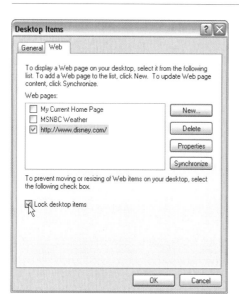

Okay, now that you've got the weather, your Internet Home Page, and bouncing balls set up on your Desktop just the way you want them, it's time to lock them in place. Again (you guessed it), right-click the Desktop and click Properties on the Shortcut menu. Next, click the Desktop tab and click Customize Desktop. Click the Web tab in the dialog box, check Lock Desktop Items, click OK, then Apply. Now, no matter what you do to your Desktop, your Web items aren't movin'.

CHANGE YOUR POINTER SCHEME

The first thing I do when I get a new computer is head straight for the cursors and change them. It's not that the default ones are bad; I've just been using the same ones forever and I'm not comfortable using anything else. If you want to change your pointer scheme, then click Start and open the Control Panel. (*Note*: Control Panel should not be in Category view.) Next, click on Printers and Other Hardware, then Mouse. In the dialog box, choose the Pointers tab and browse the available themes. Select the one that suits you, then click OK.

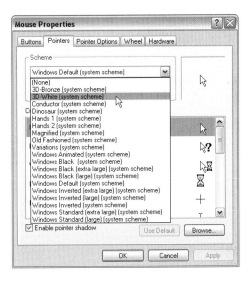

IT'S NOT EASY LOOKIN' THIS GOOD

Windows XP is a great-looking operating system; however, there's a cost for all this beauty. Windows' visual effects require processing speed that can slow your system's performance—not everyone really cares all that much about good looks. (Not me of course. I'm very shallow; all I care about is looks!)

If you're not like me, however, you can disable or customize Windows' animations. Click Start and open the Control Panel. Choose Performance and Maintenance then click System. Next, click the Advanced tab in the dialog box and then the Performance Settings button. Choose the Visual Effects tab in the dialog box and from here you can turn off many of Windows' visual effects.

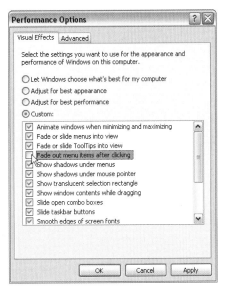

Cruisin'

NAVIGATING WINDOWS XP

I'm not sure that I know exactly how to say this, but this isn't exactly the sexiest chapter in the book. Oh, don't get me

Cruisin'

navigating windows xp

wrong. This chapter is as sexy as any chapter about navigating Windows could get. It's just that navigating Windows is plain "un-sexy." It's pretty much point-and-click and doing stuff with your mouse, although I do show some silly cool ways to do it (navigate Windows, that is). I did briefly consider using a picture of super-model Heidi Klum for my Desktop's background to liven up the screen captures, but quickly realized that was a very bad idea. (I really can't explain why it was a bad idea, it just was, and I'm very, very sorry.) So, although Heidi will not be appearing in this chapter, I'm sure you will enjoy it anway.

 IT ALL HAPPENS HERE...GET THERE QUICKLY

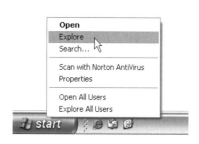

Here's a great little tip that I use daily. Windows Explorer is where you go to view everything on your computer: drives, files, folders, directories, it's all here. I'm always diggin' around in Windows Explorer, and it's handy to have a really quick way to get there. Simply right-click Start and click Explore on the Shortcut menu.

 A DIFFERENT DEFAULT VIEW

It's easy to change the default startup location of Windows Explorer. Click Start, point to All Programs>Accessories. Right-click Windows Explorer and click Properties on the Shortcut menu. Next, click the Shortcut tab, and the Target text box should read something like "%SystemRoot%\explorer.exe." To change the startup location to point to, let's say, Program Files, edit the text to this: "%SystemRoot%\explorer.exe\root, C:\Program Files" (without the quotes), and click OK. Now Explorer will open to the Program Files folder at launch. Follow this example to point Explorer to open anywhere on your hard drive.

TURN ANY WINDOW INTO EXPLORER

You can turn any open window into an Explorer window by clicking the Folders button on the Standard Buttons Toolbar. When you click the Folders button, the Tasks Panel switches to the Explorer (Folders) view.

 ## INSTANTLY EXPLORE ANY FILE

In the previous tip, we showed you how to turn any window into an Explorer window, but here's what really makes this tip useful. The next time you need to quickly explore (find the location of) a folder or file you're viewing in a window, click the Folder's button while the folder or file is highlighted. This will instantly show its location on your hard drive.

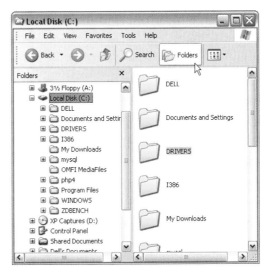

 CAN'T SEE IT? DOESN'T MATTER

If you need to move a file to a subfolder that you can't see because the parent folder isn't expanded, then drag the file to the parent folder and hold it there for a second. The folder will expand, showing its contents. Now, just drag-and-drop the file onto any subfolder.

 JUST TYPE ITS NAME

This can really come in handy when trying to locate a file in a large folder, such as My Documents. To locate a file, type the first couple of letters of the title and you'll instantly jump to documents beginning with those letters. You can even type the entire title, if necessary, to go directly to the document.

IT'S ALL ABOUT THE DETAILS

Details view is probably the best view for Windows Explorer. Details, as the name implies, gives you details about a file. By default, Explorer's Details view shows a file's name, size, type, and date modified; however, you can choose to show many other details of a file. To do this, right-click a column heading and click an available detail you want to display from the Shortcut menu. The new Details column will automatically append to the end of the existing columns.

 MAKING THE DETAILS FIT

Now that you've added 20 more columns to your Details view, it sure would be nice to actually see a column's info—it can get a little crowded. To see more of your columns, move your pointer over the separator between the column headings. When your pointer changes to the horizontal cursor, click-and-hold, then drag the separator to the left or right to resize the column.

 LET'S SORT THIS OUT

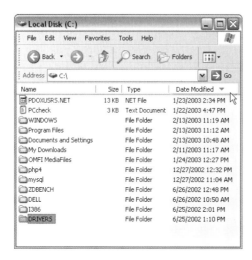

A quick way to help locate files is to sort them. Sorting lets you find a file by its alphabetical listing in the Name column, or by the date a file was created or modified from its Date Modified column. You can sort your files using any of the Details columns you have open. To sort your files, simply click a Details column, and your files sort themselves instantly.

 REARRANGE COLUMNS IN DETAILS VIEW

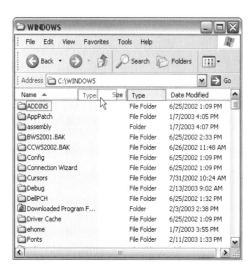

It never fails! You've added details to your folder but, of course, the most important detail is located at the end, and every time you want to view this detail you're forced to scroll all the way to your right to see it. That's a pain! Don't suffer; just rearrange your details. Click-and-hold the column heading that you want to move and drag-and-drop it in any order you want.

USING THE KEYBOARD TO NAVIGATE VIEWS

Try using the keyboard when you
need to navigate folders quickly.
You can use your Arrow keys to
move up and down and to jump
from column to column. When
you've selected the file you want
to open, press Enter.

 ## WINDOWS A MESS? GROUP 'EM

Organize your files by grouping them. Try this:
Open a folder containing several different
subfolders and file types. Right-click any empty
space on the window's Contents Pane, point to
Arrange Icons By, and click Show in Groups. To
arrange the window's contents, right-click again
in any empty space on the window's Contents
Pane, point to Arrange Icons By, and click Name,
Size, Type, or Modified.

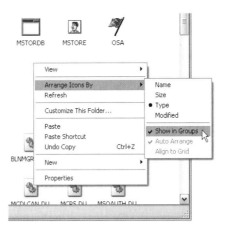

 I'M FEELING A LITTLE BLUE; I'M COMPRESSED

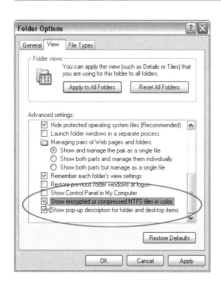

In Chapter 1, we showed you how to compress files in Windows ("You Can Make It Smaller if You Squeeze It"). You can choose to have Windows show encrypted and compressed files in color to identify them. Here's how: Click Start>My Computer>Tools>Folder Options. Next, click the View tab in the dialog box, scroll the Advanced Settings, and click Show Encrypted or Compressed NTFS Files in Color. Click OK. The text of the file's name is now blue. *Note*: Your hard drive's file system must be NTFS to use this option.

 FIND YOUR HIDDEN FILES

By default, Windows hides system files from your view—to prevent them from accidentally being deleted or moved. There are times, though, when it's necessary to view these files—usually by more advanced users who want to alter a System file. If you want to see your System and other hidden Windows files, you can. First, click Start>My Computer>Tools>Folder Options. Next, click the View tab in the dialog box, scroll the Advanced Settings, click Show Hidden Files and Folders, then click OK. Now you'll be able to see Windows' hidden files.

WHERE AM I?

Personally, I always like to know where I am in any folder, and where the files are located on my hard drive when I'm browsing. You can always view the path to any file by looking on the Address Bar Toolbar. First, click Start>My Computer>Tools>Folder Options. Next, click the View tab in the dialog box, scroll the Advanced settings, click Display the Full Path in the Address Bar, then click OK. Now open the Address Bar Toolbar by right-clicking the Standard Buttons Toolbar and clicking Address Bar. You can now see a file's and folder's full path in the window's Address Bar.

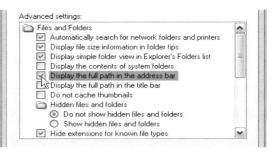

 ## WHERE AM I? (ANOTHER WAY)

There's another way to view file paths if you don't want the Address Bar Toolbar on your windows. You can view paths to your files from the Title Bar. Click Start>My Computer>Tools>Folder Options. Next, click the View tab in the dialog box, scroll the Advanced settings, click Display the full path in the Title Bar, then click OK. You can now see a file's and folder's full path on the window's Title Bar.

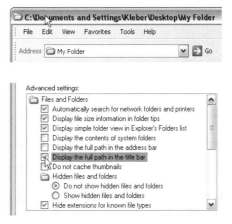

 NO GO

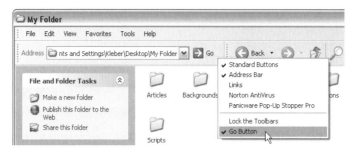

The Go button is nice, but how often do you really use it? When browsing folders—never. When browsing the Web, occasionally. I usually simply press the Enter key after typing URLs into the Address Bar Toolbar. For the most part, the Go button just takes up space, so turn it off. On the Address Bar, right-click on the Go button and click Go Button on the Shortcut menu to deselect. This removes the Go button. To get it back, right-click the Address Bar Toolbar and click the Go button again.

 DELETE THIS!

There are several ways to delete files, which is a good thing because you really can't have enough ways to delete files. Of course, you can drag-and-drop a file into the Recycle bin, or you can right-click a file and click Delete on its Shortcut menu; but there's also a couple of other ways that are quicker and more convenient. The Windows File and Folder Tasks Pane lets you delete selected files by clicking the Delete the Selected Items link. You can also put a Delete button on the Standard Buttons Toolbar.

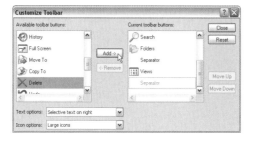

TAKING OUT THE TRASH

Now that you've deleted half your hard drive playing around with the different ways to delete a file, it's time to empty the Recycle Bin. There's no need to open the Recycle Bin to empty it, simply right-click the Recycle Bin's icon and click Empty Recycle Bin on the Shortcut menu. You'll be asked to confirm your request. Look, you just took out the trash.

 OOPS! I DIDN'T MEAN TO DELETE THAT

Okay, you've gotten careless and accidentally deleted two years' worth of family pictures taken with your digital camera. Don't panic, you can get them back. Open the Recycle Bin from the Desktop, select the accidentally deleted files, and click the Restore This Item link on the Recycle Bin Tasks Pane. You can also restore a file(s) from the Recycle Bin by first selecting the file(s) to restore, then clicking File, and clicking Restore on the Menu Bar. Another quick way to restore a deleted file—and you do this from an open folder immediately after you've deleted the file—is to press-and-hold the Ctrl key, then press the Z key. This keyboard shortcut will undelete the file(s).

 NAVIGATE WINDOWS WITHOUT THE MOUSE

If you need (or want) to navigate the items in a window without your mouse, go right ahead and use your keyboard. Pressing the Tab key will highlight items in open windows. Just keep pressing Tab to select Toolbars, Tasks Panes, and the Content Pane. Use the Arrow keys to move to available items, then press Enter to open or choose a selected item.

 NAVIGATE MENUS WITHOUT THE MOUSE

Try this keyboard tip to navigate an open window's Menu Bar: Press the Alt key and you'll notice that the first menu item on the Menu Bar (usually "File") is selected, and a small horizontal line underlining a letter of each menu item now appears. Press-and-hold the Alt key then press the menu's underlined letter on the keyboard to open the menu. Now, use the same technique to select a menu's items, then press Enter to choose the highlighted item.

SAVE IT WHERE YA' WANT IT

When you save a new file or document in
Windows, the Save dialog box usually opens
in My Documents, encouraging you to save all
your files there. I don't know about you but I
rarely want to save files to the My Documents
folder. To save your files to the location of
your choice, click File on the Menu Bar then
click Save As. In the dialog box, click the down
arrow on the Save In menu to quickly view your
hard drive. Use the Save In menu to navigate to
the location of your choice and then click Save.

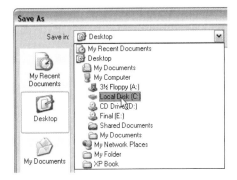

 QUICK SAVE

The next time you're saving files, check out the left panel
of the Save As dialog box—this panel has links to popular
destinations on your hard drive. Simply click any of these
buttons to quickly open the locations, give your file a name,
and click Save.

 INSTANTLY SAVE TO A NEW FOLDER

 If you're saving a file and realize that it needs to be saved to its own folder, you can do it right in the Save As dialog box. Use the Save In menu to navigate to the location on your hard drive where you want to create the new folder, then click the Create New Folder icon in the Save As dialog box. Now, a new folder appears ready to be named. Name that folder, double-click the new folder to open it, and click Save.

 SINGLE CLICK? DON'T OVERWRITE

 I'm trying to save you a lot of pain with this tip. When you have Windows set up to use a single click to open an item, be cautious not to over-write files when saving. When I have similar files or documents that I'm saving to the same folder, using similar names (for example, Jarod's Birth-day Pics 1.jpg, Jarod's Birthday Pics 2.jpg, etc.), I like to select one of the names in the Save As dialog box (this makes the name appear in the File Name field), then change the 2 to 3, 3 to 4, and so on, to number the files. When saving, this is much faster than retyping the name of each file just to add a different number.

Here's where it gets sticky: If you're using single-click in Windows, make sure you do not click the file's name (doing this will overwrite the file). Point to the file name instead of clicking—this selects the name, puts it in the File Name field, and allows you to change the file's name without overwriting. Whew!

 I DON'T THINK I'LL SAVE AFTER ALL

Decided that you didn't want to save after all? Don't click Exit on the File menu as this will close your window. Hit Esc(ape) on your keyboard instead, which closes the menu without taking any action. You can also click anywhere on the document, click File on the Menu Bar again, or just unplug your computer from the wall (kidding). Take your pick; they work equally well. Of course, this tip works for any Windows menu.

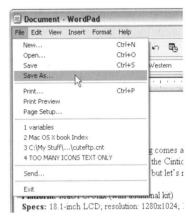

 RESIZE OPEN/SAVE DIALOG BOX

Open and Save dialog boxes can get a little tricky to navigate when there are a lot of files in a folder. To make it a little easier to see a folder's contents, resize it. Click-hold and drag any side or corner of the dialog box to make it larger. That's better! Now you can see.

 YOU CAN CUT AND PASTE FROM HERE

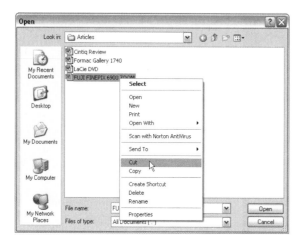

Okay, you've saved your file and realized that you put it in the wrong place. You don't have to open Windows Explorer to put it in the right spot. You can actually use the Open and Save dialog boxes to cut-and-paste the file to wherever you want. To do this, from the Open or Save dialog box, right-click the file you want to move, and click Cut on the Shortcut menu. Now, navigate to where you want to move the file on your hard drive, right-click a blank space anywhere in the folder, and click Paste from the Shortcut menu. You just moved your file!

 SHOW FILE EXTENSIONS

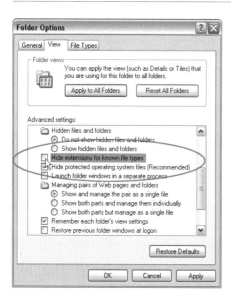

By default, Windows doesn't show the extension of known file types (.doc, .txt, .jpg, .avi, and so on). You can, however, make Windows always show a file's extension. This can be helpful when choosing a program to open a file type. Here's how to do it: Click Start>My Computer>Tools>Folder Options. Next, click the View tab in the dialog box, scroll the Advanced settings, and click on the checkbox to deselect Hide Extensions for Known File Types. Click OK. Now Windows will show a file's extension after its name.

BE CHOOSY WITH EXTENSIONS

Maybe you have no need to see all of your files' extensions all the time, but there may be an occasion when you need to view a single file's extension to help identify it. This can happen when you have more than one file type associated with a program. To see a single file's extension, click Start>My Computer>Tools>Folder Options. Next, click the File Types tab in the dialog box, scroll the Registered file types, and click the extension you always want to see. With the file selected, click Advanced, click to check Always Show Extension (at the bottom of the Edit File Type dialog box), then click OK. Now Windows will display the extension for only the selected file type.

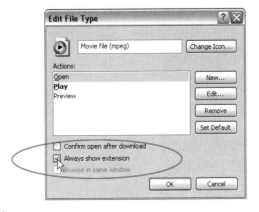

 SYSTEM PROPERTIES IN A CLICK

System Properties is probably one of the most important tools in Windows and here's a quick way to open your System Properties dialog box. While holding the Alt Key, double-click the My Computer icon on your Desktop. And there it is—System Properties in a click!

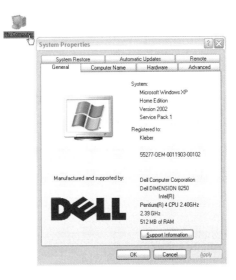

 YOU CAN ALWAYS GO BACK

When navigating through a folder's open window, you can always go back to where you started. There are several ways to do this. Click the Back button or Up button on the Standard Buttons Toolbar to move back one folder with each click. You can also use the Backspace key to navigate back one folder each time it's pressed. This comes in handy when a window's Toolbars aren't visible.

 MOVING FILES USING THE TASKS PANE

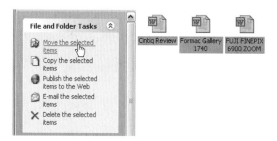

To quickly move or copy files from an open window to any location on your hard drive, simply highlight the file(s) and click the Move This File or Copy This File link in the Windows File and Folder Tasks Pane. This opens a dialog box that allows you to select a location on your hard drive. After you've navigated to the new location, click Move or Copy in the dialog box, and your file's now in its new location.

An American Icon

WORKING WITH ICONS

This chapter is named "An American Icon," not "American Idol." So, all of you out there who clearly cannot sing, please don't

An American Icon

working with icons in windows xp

send me an audition tape. What's the matter with some of those people? Really, don't they know how shockingly bad their singing is? Don't they have friends or family who would care enough to smack them on the head with a hammer rather than let them walk out the door to audition? I'd rather swallow sandspurs than be a judge for that show. Anyway, this chapter is about icons. I know, you're thinking, "Icons?" Yeah, icons. Don't dismiss them or you could miss a lot. Just about everything in XP is icon-related, and this chapter shows you what they're all about and how to do cool things with 'em. And the best thing about icons—they don't sing!

 ## SEND SHORTCUTS TO THE DESKTOP

Don't you hate looking for frequently used programs through the All Programs menu? Me too! End the frustration and put a shortcut icon to your favorite Apps on your Desktop. Click the Start button and point to All Programs. Browse the menu and select a program. Right-click the program's icon, point to Send To, and click Desktop (Create Shortcut) on the Shortcut menu; or simply drag-and-drop the icon onto your Desktop. You now have a shortcut icon to the program on your Desktop.

 ## MOVE FOLDERS

You can easily move folders back and forth from window to window, or from a window to the Desktop, or...(you get the picture) by clicking-and-holding the folder's icon and simply dragging-and-dropping it to a new location.

DRAG-AND-DROP SHORTCUTS

If you want to create a shortcut to a folder, click-and-hold the folder's icon with your mouse and drag it to a new location in the same window, Desktop, or wherever (don't let go of it), then press and hold the Alt key. You'll notice that the icon you're dragging now has a shortcut arrow on it. While still holding the Alt key, drop the icon. You just created a shortcut to your folder.

 DRAG-AND-DROP COPIES

You can also use the previous technique to create a copy of a folder, but press-and-hold the Ctrl key as you drop the icon. This creates an exact copy of your folder and all of its contents.

 CAN'T MAKE UP YOUR MIND? GIVE YOURSELF OPTIONS

If you're not sure exactly what you want to do with a shortcut or folder, then drag-and-drop it using the right-mouse button. Press the right-mouse button, grab your icon and drag-and-drop it; when you let go, a Shortcut menu will pop up with several choices. Now you can take your time deciding whether you want to move the icon, copy it, or create a shortcut to it.

 CREATE SHORTCUTS FROM THE START MENU

The Start menu offers links to many of the most popular locations on your computer (My Documents, Control Panel, Search, and so on), and you might be tempted to put a shortcut to them on your Desktop. Well, it's easy! Click Start, then click-and-hold any menu item, and drag-and-drop it onto the Desktop.

 CREATE A SHORTCUT FOR JUST ABOUT ANYTHING

There's another way to create a shortcut: Right-click the Desktop or empty space inside an open window's Contents Pane, point to New, and then click Shortcut. The Shortcut Wizard will open and ask you to browse your hard drive and locate the program or folder for which you want to create a shortcut. Once you've provided the location, click Next, name your shortcut, then click Finish.

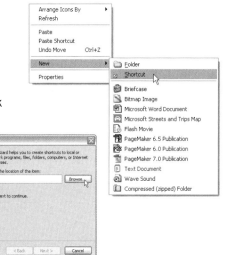

 DON'T FORGET THE SHORTCUT'S SHORTCUT MENU

You might think that you wouldn't have a Shortcut menu for a short-cut, but you do—it's just slightly different from its target. So, you still have access to many of the same timesaving links on the shortcut's Shortcut menu that you'd have on the target's Shortcut menu. (Whew, that's got to be a record for the most times the word shortcut has ever been used in a paragraph.)

 I KNOW IT'S A SHORTCUT

I'm not sure why Windows automatically puts the words "Shortcut to" before the title of each shortcut. I mean, I know it's a shortcut. I just made it and it's got that annoying arrow on it. Well, you can delete those words and rename the shortcut to whatever you'd like, even the same as the target. Your computer won't crash or instantly delete files—even your computer knows it's a shortcut.

 CHANGE A SHORTCUT'S ICON

Hey, don't you just love default application icons? I think there's just one guy who makes all icons—and he doesn't have a sense of humor—so, let's change them. Right-click the shortcut and click Properties on the Shortcut menu. Next, click the Shortcut tab in the dialog box and click Change Icon. Then, browse your hard drive to select a new icon and click OK. Click Apply and you'll see your new icon.

CHANGE A FOLDER'S ICON

Did you know that when you create any new folders, they're all represented by exactly the same icon—a little boring, eh? We can change their icons, though, and here's how. Right-click a folder, click Properties on the Shortcut menu, then click the Customize tab in the dialog box. Click Change Icon, browse your hard drive to select a new icon, and then click OK. Click Apply and you'll see your new icon.

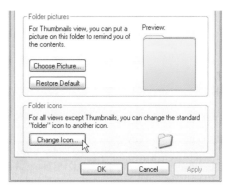

 ## DON'T LIKE YOUR NEW ICON? CHANGE IT BACK

If you've changed a folder's icon and realized that the new icon is just plain bad (as in not good), you can always restore the original icon. Right-click the folder's icon, click Properties on the Shortcut menu, and then the Customize tab in the dialog box. Click Change Icon, click Restore Defaults, then click Apply, and your old icon's back.

 MAKE YOUR OWN ICONS

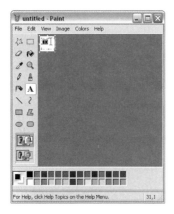

It's shockingly easy to create your own icons in XP. Let's do it: Click Start, point to All Programs, then to Accessories, and click Paint. Click Image on the Menu Bar, then click Attributes. Type 32 for both the Width and Height of the document, and make sure that Pixels is selected under Units. Click OK to create a new 32x32-pixel document: the size of an icon.

Now add type, color, or do whatever you'd like to your image. I like to shrink photos (headshots work best) to 32x32 and simply paste them into my Paint document. When you're finished, click File (on the Menu Bar), then Save As. Use the dialog box to choose where you want to save your file, then give it a name followed by ".ico" (without the quotes), and click Save. (The extension ".ico" tells Windows that it's an icon file.) You just created an icon! Now you can change any shortcut or folder to your own icon, just browse to it on your hard drive.

 ARRANGE YOUR ICONS

You can quickly arrange your Desktop and folder icons by right-clicking empty space on your Desktop or an open folder's Contents Pane. Now point to Arrange Icons By, and then click Name, Size, Type, or Modified on the Shortcut menu.

KEEP YOUR ICONS IN LINE

If your icons just won't stay in line, try putting them on a grid. To do this, right-click empty space on your Desktop or an open folder's Contents Pane, point to Arrange Icons By, then click Align to Grid on the Shortcut menu. Now your icons will automatically snap to an invisible grid, so no matter where you move them, they'll stay evenly spaced from one another.

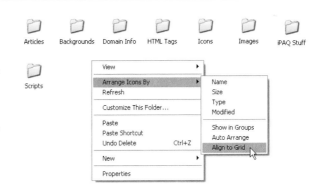

ADJUST ICON SPACING

If the default spacing of your icons just doesn't give you enough room for comfort, you can increase the spacing to give your icons a bit more elbowroom and extra space for long file names.

Right-click the Desktop and click Properties on the Shortcut menu. Next, click the Appearance tab then click Advanced. Select Icon Spacing (Horizontal) on the Item drop-down menu, change the Size to a larger number (up to 150 pixels), then click OK. Click Apply and your Desktop will refresh, displaying the new spacing between icons. To adjust vertical spacing between your icons, do the same thing for Icon Spacing (Vertical).

 ## WHERE ARE MY DESKTOP ICONS?

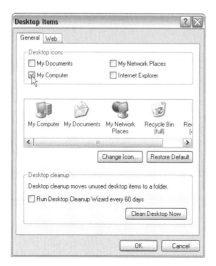

By default, Windows XP now shows only the Recycle Bin's icon on the Desktop, but you can get your old familiar items like My Computer, My Documents, and other icons back. Right-click the Desktop, click Properties on the Shortcut menu, and then click the Desktop tab in the dialog box. Next, click Customize Desktop and click the General tab. Now, check the Desktop icons that you want to appear and click OK.

You can also quickly add icons back to the Desktop: Right-click My Computer or My Network Places on the Start menu and select Show on Desktop on the Shortcut menu.

 ## CHANGE DEFAULT DESKTOP ICONS

Windows' default Desktop icons (My Computer, My Documents, My Network Places, and Recycle Bin) cannot be changed using their Shortcut menus, and this might make you think that you just can't do it—but you can.

Right-click the Desktop, click Properties, then click on the Desktop tab, and then Customize Desktop. Click the General tab, select a default Desktop icon to change, and click Change Icon. Select a new icon, then click OK. Do this for any or all of the default icons. When you're finished, click OK, then Apply.

SUPER-SIZE 'EM

Want to try something really
freaky? Right-click the
Desktop and click Properties
on the Shortcut menu. Next,
click the Appearance tab in
the dialog box, then click
Advanced. Select Icon on the
Item drop-down menu and
change the Size from 32 to 72
(pixels). Click OK, then Apply.
Isn't that freaky? Icons the
size of your fist, weird!

DELL

Internet
Explorer

Photoshop

 CREATE A NEW FOLDER

To create a new folder, right-click the Desktop
or empty space in an open folder's Content
Pane, point to New, then click Folder on the
Shortcut menu. You can also click the Make a
New Folder link in the File and Folder
Tasks Pane.

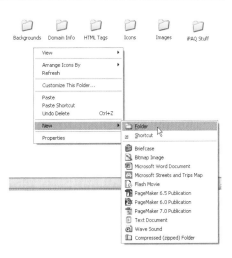

ADD COMMENTS TO YOUR SHORTCUT ICONS

Have you ever created a shortcut some time back and now can't remember what it was to or what it was for? To help prevent this from happening in the future, you can put comments on your shortcuts. Right-click a shortcut's icon and click Properties on the Shortcut menu. Next, click the Shortcut tab in the dialog box and type any comments, descriptions, or reminders in the Comment text field, then click OK. Now, when you move your pointer over the shortcut's icon, a description pops up displaying your comments.

LOCATE A SHORTCUT'S TARGET

To locate a shortcut's target, right-click the shortcut and click Properties on the Shortcut menu. Next, click the Shortcut tab in the dialog box and look in the Target text field. This field shows the location of the shortcut's target file or folder on your hard drive.

THAT'S A LONG FILE NAME

It's pretty cool that you can give any file a name as long as a paragraph in XP, but have you noticed that as soon as you deselect the file, its 200-word title now has about three words followed by "..."? So much for the most descriptive title in history. Well, the full name is still there; XP just hides it until you need it, which is actually a pretty good thing. When you want to see your title in full again, simply scroll over or single-click the file to select it. This will once again display the file's title in full.

TURN ON THE THUMBNAILS

The Thumbnails view (View>Thumbnails) is extremely useful when viewing photos, but the view also helps you to identify other file types quickly. Try opening a folder containing various file types and select View>Thumbnails. Take a look around and you can quickly see photos, movie clips, documents, and other file types—I could get used to this.

 SELECT EVERYTHING IN A FOLDER

   There are a couple of ways to select everything in a folder; for example, you can use the keyboard: Press-and-hold Ctrl-A to select every item in a folder.

 CLICK-AND-DRAG TO SELECT ICONS

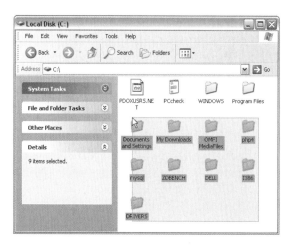

You can also click-and-drag a box around all of the items in a folder to select them. Once you've dragged your box over the items, let go of the mouse button and everything will be selected.

SELECT ALMOST EVERYTHING

If you want to select just about everything in a folder, try this:
Use the previous techniques to select your files, then press-and-hold the Ctrl key and scroll over (or single-click) to deselect each file that you don't want.

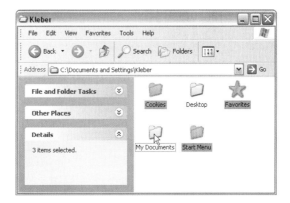

SELECT CONTINUOUS/NONCONTINUOUS FILES

To select continuous files (top image), click on the first file you want to select, then press-and-hold the Shift key. Move your pointer to the last file that you want to select and scroll over it (or single-click) with your mouse, and all files in between are automatically selected. You can also click-and-drag over the continuous files you want selected.

To select noncontinuous files (bottom), press-and-hold the Ctrl key and point to (or single-click) each file that you want to select.

Fast & Furious

WINDOWS XP SPEED TIPS

This chapter isn't actually furious, but it is fast. Well, not like racecar fast—that would just be plain silly. I mean think

The Fast and The Furious

windows xp speed tips

about it: If the chapter were racecar fast, like jump-off-the-page and run-around-your-room kind of fast, it would be pretty difficult to read, and that would just completely defeat the purpose of the chapter. I mean, you do want to read the chapter, right? You probably wouldn't have bought this book if the chapters were too fast to read. But wait, we're getting completely off the subject. These are Windows tips to make you faster. Well, they don't actually make you faster. You're not going to read this chapter, then run the mile in two minutes or anything like that. Is a two-minute mile even possible? Probably not, although, wasn't there a Disney movie where a guy ran faster than a cheetah, or am I thinking of a movie about a cheetah that ran faster than a guy? I wonder what can run a two-minute mile. I bet nothing can—that's pretty fast. Oh yeah, fast. This chapter is loaded with fast Windows tips. You're gonna love it.

 DRAGGING FILES TO THE RECYCLE BIN WHEN IT'S HIDDEN

Okay, you've got folders open all over the place and your Recycle Bin is buried. And you've got files to delete. You could just select the files and hit Delete on your keyboard—but where's the fun in that? Try this drag-and-drop tip instead: Select the files you want to delete, then click-and-drag them to a blank spot on your Taskbar. Keep holding down the mouse button, hold your mouse there for a couple of seconds, and all of your open windows will minimize. Now, just drop your files in the Recycle Bin.

 A QUICKER WAY TO RENAME

iPAQ Stuff   Scripts

Renaming a file is already pretty quick and painless in Windows; however, if you want to rename your files even faster—and who doesn't—try this: Single-click or move your cursor over the file or icon to highlight it; once it's highlighted, hit F2. This keyboard shortcut selects the icon's text and quickly renames it.

UNDO RENAMING MISTAKES

If you're like me, you'll
never need this tip. We
never make spelling
mistakes, right? Actually,
I make mistakes all the
time; I'm just comfort-
able living with them.
But for those who care
about spelling, here ya'
go. You've just begun
to rename a file and,
of course, completely
botched the spelling. Just

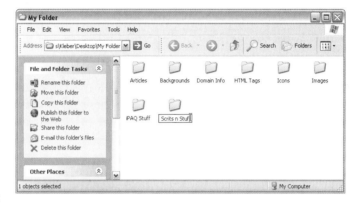

hit the Esc key while your text cursor is still active, and the file's name is restored to its
original spelling; then rename it correctly.

 E-MAIL ATTACHMENTS FROM JUST ABOUT ANYWHERE

Here's a really handy tip. Locate a file
anywhere on your hard drive that you want
to e-mail, right-click the file's icon, point
to Send To, and click Mail Recipient on the
Shortcut menu. A new mail message will
open with the file attached and ready to
send. But what's really speedy about this tip
is that your mail program doesn't launch.
This action creates only a single new mail
message. Now, to send your attachment,
simply type the recipient's e-mail address
in the To text field, add any accompanying
message, then click the Send icon. The subject
and attachment fields are already set.

 COOL! TOOLBAR DRIVES

I use this tip every day: Placing a shortcut to drives on your Links Toolbar makes copying files to CD, or any other drive, quick and convenient from any window. Here's how. Click Start>My Computer, then right-click the Standard Buttons Toolbar and click Links on the Shortcut menu. Next, click-and-drag a drive to the Links Toolbar and let go. Now, no matter which window you're in, you can drag-and-drop files to this drive or any other drive you've placed on the Toolbar.

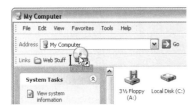

 MAKING FAVORITES A REAL FAVORITE

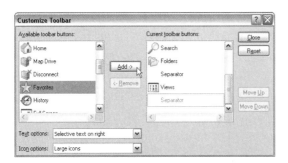

One of the really cool things about Windows is the ability to browse the Web from any open window. So, why not take full advantage of this and put Favorites on your Standard Buttons Toolbar? Click Start>My Computer, then right-click the Standard Buttons Toolbar and click Customize on the Shortcut menu. Scroll the Toolbar buttons on the left, click to highlight Favorites, click Add, and then click Close. Click the Favorites icon on the Toolbar to show the Favorites Panel. Now, you can just drag-and-drop URLs from the Address Bar to the Favorites Panel.

 SPEED LAUNCH YOUR FAVORITE APPS

Of all the programs installed on my computer, I use maybe five regularly, and it helps to be able to access these five as quickly as possible. Creating a keyboard shortcut is a great way to launch them fast. Ready? Right-click an application's shortcut icon and click Properties on the Shortcut menu. Next, click the Shortcut tab, locate the Shortcut Key text box, and type in a letter, number, or assign an F key (for letters and numbers, Windows adds Ctrl-Alt to your shortcut). Now your favorite App is just a keystroke away.

 NOT JUST NO; NO TO ALL

This tip could have easily been included in the annoying Windows stuff (Chapter 1). Have you ever wondered why Microsoft would let you select Yes to All when overwriting files but not No to All? Me too—baffling isn't it? Anyway here's how to stick it to the engineers of this little programming blunder. Hold down the Shift key and click No when asked. This keyboard trick turns No into No to All.

 OPEN MULTIPLE FILES AT THE SAME TIME

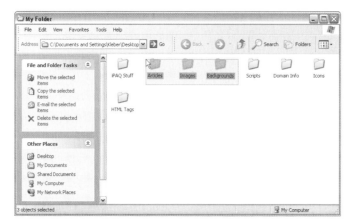

Select the files or folders you want to open and press Enter. All of the selected files open instantly. This tip will even open folders and launch applications at the same time. For example, you've selected two folders and a Word document; when you hit Enter, the two folders will open, and Word will launch to display the selected document.

 SHOW THE DESKTOP FAST; RESTORE IT EVEN FASTER

There are a couple of ways to show the Desktop. Here's my favorite with a twist. To get to your Desktop in a hurry, simply click the Show Desktop icon located in the Quick Launch Toolbar. This minimizes all open windows to display your Desktop. Now for the twist: To restore your Desktop, click the Show Desktop icon again and your windows will be restored exactly as they were.

 ## SHORTCUT TO SHUT DOWN

Is it just me or does it require way too
many mouse clicks to shut down your
computer? By my count, it's three. If
Microsoft had really given it some thought,
I'm sure they could have added a fourth
click somewhere. Please, keep it coming!
I love carpal tunnel! Just for the fun of
it, though, let's see if we can't shut down
a little faster. Right-click your Desktop,
point to New, and click Shortcut on the
Shortcut menu. In the Type the Location
of the Item text box, type "%windir%\
System32\shutdown.exe -s -t 0" (without

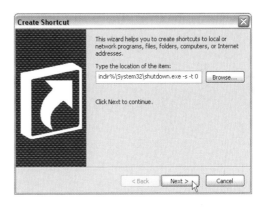

the quotes), then click Next. Give your new shortcut a name and click Finish. You now have
a Desktop icon that shuts down your computer with a single click.

 ## SWITCH 'EM OUT AND LOCK 'EM UP

This tip falls in line with the whole three-
click shutdown controversy. Did you know
that it also takes three clicks of the mouse
to switch users? Crazy, isn't it? Anyway,
we're going to fix this wonderful bit of
thoughtful programming with another
Desktop shortcut. Right-click your Desktop, point to New, and click Shortcut on
the Shortcut menu. In the Type the Location of the Item text box, type "%windir%\
System32\rundll32.exe user32.dll,
LockWorkStation" (without the quotes),
then click Next. Give your new shortcut
a name and click Finish. You now have a
Desktop icon that allows you to quickly
switch users and a great way to instantly
lock your computer.

 A USEFUL POWER BUTTON?

I rarely ever shut down my computer; instead, I tend to Hibernate my system. Here's a clever way to speed up this task and make your computer's Power button Hibernate for you. Click Start and open the Control Panel. Click the Performance and Maintenance icon, then click the Power Options icon. Click the Advanced tab and select Hibernate from the Power Buttons drop-down menu. Now, when you push your computer's Power button, your system will immediately Hibernate.

 QUICK QUITTING

Tired of chasing down the Close Window icon to exit active windows? Then try using the keyboard—it's faster and, well, just plain fun. Okay, it's not really fun, but it is faster. Hold down the Ctrl key and then press F4 to close active windows. Oh yeah, don't worry if a file needs to be saved, you'll be prompted to save your document before the window closes.

INSTANTLY RESIZE COLUMNS IN DETAIL VIEW

There's an easy way to instantly adjust columns in Detail view to auto-fit the columns' contents; however, it's not obvious. Put your mouse on the separator between the columns—you'll get a cross cursor with left and right arrows. Double-click when this cursor pops up and the column will automatically resize to fit the column's contents; or press Ctrl-+ (plus) to adjust all of the headers at once.

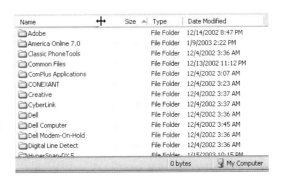

QUICKLY EXPAND FOLDERS

There are few things more tedious in Windows Explorer than clicking the little plus (+) symbol to expand or contract folders. So don't. Try this instead: Click any folder or directory in Windows Explorer, then press the asterisk (*) key on the number keypad. This instantly expands every sub-folder. Press the minus key to instantly contract the folder or directory. That's easier, isn't it?

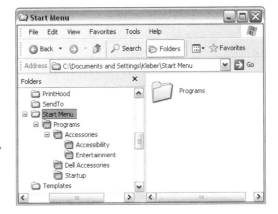

 DON'T FORGET ME, I'M SPECIAL

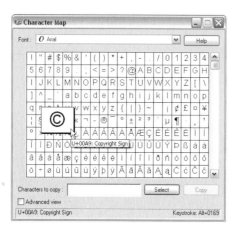

There are probably one or two special characters that you use regularly (for example, ® and ©). It can be a real time-waster to open your Character Map every time you want to insert one of these symbols. So don't! Open the Character Map by clicking Start, pointing to All Programs, and then Accessories. Point to System Tools and click Character Map. Click the © symbol. Notice that the bottom-right corner of the Character Map shows the keyboard shortcut used to insert the special character. Write it down for later use. When you want to insert that character, here's the trick: Position the cursor where you want to insert the special character, then with Num Lock on, hold down the Alt key and use the number pad keys to type the Unicode character value.

 LAUNCH FAVORITE APPS AT STARTUP

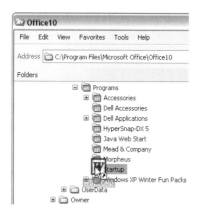

Are there programs that you open as soon as your computer boots up—like Word? Wouldn't it be nice if Windows could just open Word for you automatically at startup? You, my friend, are in luck—Windows can.

Right-click Start and click Explore on the Shortcut menu. Navigate to your Startup folder, usually located at C:\Documents and Settings\Your User Name\Start Menu\Programs\Startup. Now, just drag-and-drop an App's icon into your Startup folder to create a shortcut to it. When Windows starts up, the program will launch automatically. You can also put shortcuts to your favorite folders in Startup to have them launch instantly.

ONE-CLICK PROPERTIES

Instead of right-clicking a folder and clicking Properties on the Shortcut menu, try this tip the next time you need to view a folder's Properties. Hold the Alt key and click the folder. (You can also use double-click, if that's your style.) Now, that's faster!

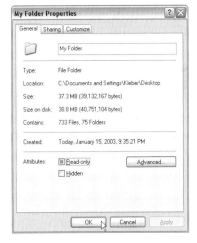

 ## TOGGLE OPEN ITEMS ON THE TASKBAR

This tip works great when you have several documents open at the same time. As with Microsoft Word and most other applications, every time you open a new document, a Taskbar button is created. The Taskbar can get pretty difficult to navigate when this happens. A quick way to maneuver is to hold the Alt key and press the Esc key. This will toggle items on the Taskbar and bring each open document to the foreground as it's selected.

YOU CAN BE CHOOSY WHEN OPENING FILES

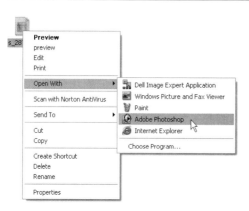

You've just downloaded photos from your digital camera. By default, JPEGs are associated with Windows Picture and Fax Viewer; so, if you click a photo, it will open in Picture and Fax Viewer. But what if you don't just want to view the photos, you want to make changes to them? Well, you can quickly choose a different program to open the photo without changing the file's association. Here's how: Right-click the file's icon, point to Open With, and click the App you want to open the file. If you don't see your program listed, click Choose Program to locate it.

DELETE AN OPEN FOLDER?

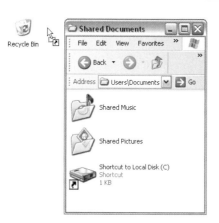

I know, you're thinking that I've lost my mind. You can't delete an open folder, right? Wrong, you sure can. In an open folder, click-and-hold the folder's icon on the folder's Title Bar, and drag it to your Recycle Bin. You just deleted an open folder. Cool!

CREATE A SHORTCUT OF AN OPEN FOLDER

Many times, you don't actually
realize that you need a shortcut to
a folder until it's open and you're
working in it. Wouldn't it be great
if you could create a shortcut to
it right then and there? You can!
From an open folder, click-and-
hold the folder's icon located on
the folder's Title Bar, and just
drag it to your Desktop. A shortcut
from an open folder—can it get
any better? I really don't think so.

 OPEN AN OPEN FOLDER'S SHORTCUT MENU

Okay, I've got one more open-folder tip. Hey, if you can
delete an open folder and create a shortcut from an open
folder, I don't see any reason why you shouldn't be able to view
an open folder's Shortcut menu. It makes perfect sense to me.
Just right-click the open folder's icon located on the Title Bar,
and there it is.

 YOU DON'T HAVE TO SEE IT TO MOVE IT

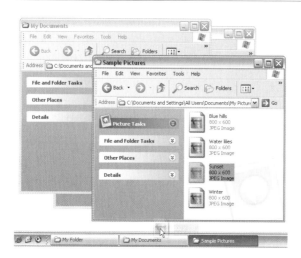

Have you ever wanted to drag-and-drop files between open windows, but you couldn't because the destination window was buried behind other open windows? Sure, we all have, but there's a way around this problem. Grab your files with your mouse, drag them to an open window's Title Bar, and let go. Problem solved!

 YOU DON'T HAVE TO SEE IT TO MOVE IT (*TAKE 2*)

The previous tip works great if you can see the destination window's Title Bar, but what do you do if you can't see any part of the window, including its Title Bar? Using your mouse, grab the files and drag them to the destination window's Taskbar button. Hold it there for a second and the window will pop to the Desktop's foreground. Now, move your mouse to the window and drop your files.

 SELECTIVELY GROUP OPEN WINDOWS ON THE TASKBAR

You've got three Internet Explorer windows open, two Word documents, and a couple of folders. Of these seven windows, you're using only three. A quick way to close the unwanted windows is to hold the Ctrl key and click the unwanted windows' Taskbar buttons to group them. Once you've selected your makeshift group, you can right-click any selected button to close, tile, minimize—you get the picture—the windows at the same time using the Shortcut menu. You can also click a button again to deselect it.

 COPY AND DELETE AT THE SAME TIME

Often, when you're moving files to a different drive (disc partition, ZIP, or CD), you're doing just that—moving them. But for some reason, Windows assumes that you actually want to copy the files instead. So, unfortunately you're forced to go back and delete the files from their original location once you've moved them. To avoid this, hold the Shift key while dragging the files to the other drives. This will move the files while deleting them at the same time from their original location.

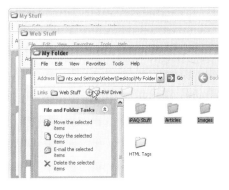

IT'S OUTTA HERE!

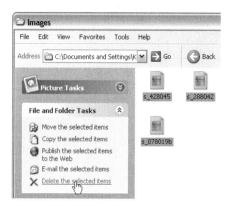

Have you ever had a file that was so repulsive, so hideous, that you just couldn't delete it fast enough? I mean a file that's so bad, even the Recycle Bin's too good for it! You have? Then try this tip the next time you need to delete an offensive file. Hold down the Shift key and press Delete, or hold down the Shift key and drag the file to the Recycle Bin. This tip deletes the file without sending it to the Recycle Bin.

I DIDN'T WANT TO DRAG THAT

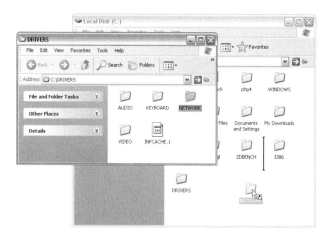

Here's a great little tip for those of us who can't seem to make up our minds. If you're dragging a file to a location and decide you really don't want to move the file after all, simply hit the Esc key on your keyboard before you let go of the mouse button and your file will magically (well, it's not really magic) return to its original location.

CLOSE A GROUP OF WINDOWS WITH ONE CLICK

If your folders open in separate windows, you know how cluttered your Desktop can get. This tip will make it a bit quicker to clean up. To close a group of windows opened from the same folder, hold the Shift key and click the Close icon on the active window's Title Bar. All windows close with a single click.

 ## CLOSE A GROUP OF WINDOWS WITH ONE CLICK
(*BUT LEAVE THE ACTIVE WINDOW OPEN*)

You're probably thinking the previous tip is great, but you're probably also thinking, "How do I leave the active window open?" After all, you had to open 10 folders to find the one you wanted. It's easy. Hold down the Shift key and click the Close icon on the folder immediately *behind* the active window. This will close all of the grouped windows except the active window.

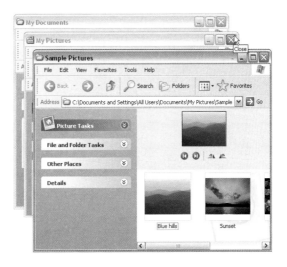

 MINIMIZE ALL WINDOWS AT ONCE

   If you don't use the Quick Launch Toolbar, you're not going to have an icon to click to show your Desktop; however, you don't need one. Hold down the Windows key on your keyboard and press the M key. This keyboard shortcut will minimize all open windows at once.

 DIDN'T MEAN TO MOVE IT? UNDO IT

   You just moved several files and suddenly you realize, "Hey, this isn't what I wanted to do at all." Well relax; we can fix this. Here's a tip to send them back to where they came from. While still in the window where you moved the misguided files, press-and-hold the Ctrl key and then press Z. This will Undo your move and return the files to their original location.

A FASTER WAY TO SEARCH FOLDERS

When I've misplaced a file, I almost always know which folder it's in, but it's usually lost in a maze of documents or buried in a subfolder. I just can't remember which subfolder. This is a great way to search a folder quickly. Locate the folder where you think the file's located, right-click the folder, and click Search on the Shortcut menu. A Search window will open, ready to search for the selected folder and only that folder. This is much quicker than launching Search and navigating your hard drive to the folder.

 DELETE THE ENTIRE WORD

I use this quick tip so often that I figured it should definitely be in this book. It doesn't happen often, but occasionally I misspell a word (actually it happens all the time!). Instead of fumbling around with the arrow keys or your mouse to move back and correct single letters, try this. Press Ctrl-Backspace, which quickly deletes the word. Now, just start over. This tip works in just about every text editor, but it doesn't work in Notepad.

We Will Rock You

ROCKIN'

WINDOWS TIPS

Woo Hoo! We will rock you! With a title like that, you just know this chapter's gonna be good—we'll show some of XP's

We Will Rock You

rockin' windows tips

best tips, tricks, and hidden Apps. You'll discover all kinds of things you just didn't know you could do in XP. Or then again you may know every single one of these tips and find this chapter completely useless. If that's the case, then please stop whatever you're doing, turn off your computer, and go to a park, Disney, the beach, or anything, because man, you've just got to get out more. Is your computer attached to your chest with fanny packs and Ace bandages? It's just a computer. The Off button is there for a reason. Good grief, use it!

For the rest of you, it won't take fanny packs, Ace bandages, and 20 hours a day to learn this stuff, because you were smart enough to buy this book. For the other guy, please get some sun, you're not looking very good.

RENAME 'EM ALL AT ONCE

If you import digital photos, you're going to love this tip. Open the folder where you've saved your pictures. Select your first batch of pictures to rename. Right-click the first picture selected and click Rename on the Shortcut menu. Rename the first picture to whatever you like (for example, Boston Vacation), then click any empty space within the window to deselect the pictures. Your pictures automatically rename themselves (Boston Vacation1, Boston Vacation2, etc.). Now, that's sweet! This tip also works to rename any collection of files.

IT'S SHOW TIME!

Boston Vacation

What's better than showing off digital pictures of your kids on the computer? Showing them as a slideshow! Here's how: Open the folder holding your photos and click the View as a Slide Show link in the Picture Tasks Pane. This creates a full-screen slide show of all the pictures in the folder.

COOL CUSTOM SCREEN SAVERS

You can also create a custom screen-saver slide show from a folder of photos. Right-click the Desktop, click Properties on the Shortcut menu, and then click the Screen Saver tab in the dialog box. Next, select My Pictures Slideshow on the Screen Saver drop-down menu. Click Settings, then click the Use Pictures in This Folder Browse button to select the location of your pictures folder, and click OK.

 ## DON'T STAND BY, HIBERNATE

You've probably noticed that Hibernate isn't an option when you turn off your computer—actually, it is! Hold down the Shift key while the Turn Off Computer dialog box is visible, and Stand By becomes Hibernate. Why it's not a permanently visible option, I don't know (and I'm sure I never will).

Why is Hibernation cool? When your computer enters Hibernation, everything in memory is saved. The next time your computer is powered-up, programs, windows, and documents that were open at the time of Hibernation are restored exactly as they were on the Desktop.

LET WINDOWS DO THE TALKING

Have you ever wondered what Windows would sound like if it could talk? Well, wonder no more; turn on Windows Narrator and let Windows talk to you. Click Start, point to All Programs, point to Accessories, to Accessibility, then click Narrator. You can set up Narrator to read menus, shortcut menus, or new windows. Narrator will even read characters aloud as you type in various Windows text editors.

GIVE THE SCRAPS TO YOUR DESKTOP

Document Scraps are one of the coolest tools in Windows. I use them all the time, especially when writing. Try this next time you're writing in a program such as Word, Notepad, or WordPad. Highlight a block of text and then drag-and-drop it onto your Desktop. You just created a Document Scrap. Now, you can drag-and-drop the Scrap back onto any of your documents at any time—a great way to save ideas and then drop them into documents when appropriate.

DRAG-AND-DROP DRIVES

I'm always accessing my drives, whether it's a floppy, CD/RW, or Zip drive, and it's convenient to have them where I can access them quickly from just about anywhere. Try putting a shortcut to them on your Desktop. Click Start>My Computer, then click-and-hold a drive's icon, and drag-and-drop it onto your Desktop. Now, you can quickly drag-and-drop files to your drives right on your Desktop.

 ## PERSONALIZE THE ALL PROGRAMS MENU

Here's something to keep in mind about the All Programs menu: The icons on the All Programs menu are only shortcuts. You can rename them, move them, or even delete them without harming the program. This means that it might also make sense to organize them to better suit you.

For instance, you could create a new All Programs folder named Design Apps to hold shortcuts to all of your graphic design programs, such as Photoshop, QuarkXPress, and Illustrator. Here's how to do it. Right-click Start, click Explore on the Shortcut menu, and navigate to your Programs folder (usually

located at C:\Documents and Settings\All Users\Start Menu\Programs). You can create new folders and move existing program folders or shortcut icons into them to sort your programs. Now when you click Start and point to All Programs, you'll see your new customized menu, making it much easier to locate your programs.

 I'M REALLY GOOD AT CHECKERS

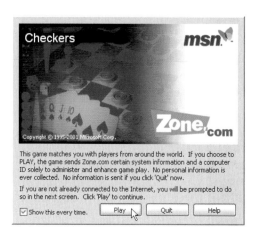

Actually I am pretty good at Checkers, but you should see me wreak havoc online. I'm tattooing people left and right. Okay, I've only played twice, but I dominated both times. XP lets you play games online against people from all over the world, and it's really easy! Click Start and point to All Programs, then point to Games and choose from five different Internet games. Checkers is my favorite—honestly, only because I'm terrible at the other ones. Anyway, make sure you're online and click the Internet game you want to play. Follow the onscreen instructions, and you're playin' Checkers against an eleven-year-old Uzbekistani, and you're whippin'-up on him. Heck, he's only eleven and he can't read English, but that doesn't mean that you shouldn't take him down.

 RIGHT-CLICK PRINT

If you need to print a document, let's say a Word document, there's no need to launch Word first. Browse your hard drive for the file that you want to print, right-click its icon, and click Print on the Shortcut menu. This will automatically send the document to your printer without launching Word.

GRANDMA'S GETTIN' A FAX

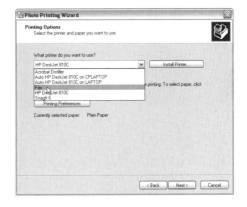

Grandma doesn't have a computer to e-mail little Jenna's pictures to, but she's got a fax. (Why Grandma has a fax and not a computer, I don't know. This is fiction; go with it.) To fax a picture quickly, right-click the photo's icon and click Print. This will open the Photo Printing Wizard. Click Next, select the picture(s) you want to fax, and click Next, which takes you to the Printing Options. Now here's the trick: On the drop-down menu where the dialog box asks, What Printer Do You Want to Use? select Fax and click Next. Choose the layout for your photo(s) and click Next. This opens the Send Fax Wizard. The Send Fax Wizard will walk you through setting up your fax, (recipient name, phone number, and so on). When you're done, click Finish. Grandma's gettin' a fax! This also works for any document you'd want to fax.

JUST GO HOME

Put the Home button on your Standard Buttons Toolbar, and you'll always have a quick link to the Web. Just click your Home button and your Internet home page launches in the open window.

Here's how to do it: Right-click the Standard Buttons Toolbar and click Customize on the Shortcut menu. Scroll the Available Toolbar Buttons, click to highlight the Home button, then click Add and Close. Now your Internet home page is only a click away.

 SEARCH THE WEB AT ANY TIME, FROM ANY PLACE

Any time you need to search the Web, simply type your question in the Address Bar of any open folder's window and hit Go or press Enter. Windows will search the Web and return the results in the open window. To put the Address Bar on your Toolbar, right-click the Standard Buttons Toolbar and click Address on the Shortcut menu.

 INSTALL FONTS WITHOUT INSTALLING THEM

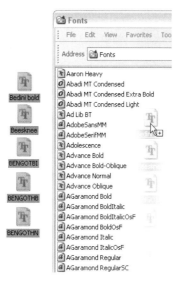

To install a new font, click Start>Control Panel, then click Appearance and Themes. Click the Fonts link on the See Also Tasks Pane, click File on the Fonts folder Menu Bar, and click Install New Font. Now, use the install dialog box to search your hard drive, select your fonts, and click install.

Whew, that seems like a lot of work, especially when you can just drag-and-drop your fonts into the Fonts folder instead. Yep, that's right, now you can just drag-and-drop fonts into the Fonts folder, and they're installed and ready to use.

NO ADOBE TYPE MANAGER? NO PROBLEM

This isn't so much a tip as it is just a great big YEAH! Previous versions of Windows couldn't install Post-Script fonts, so you had to have a program, such as ATM (Adobe Type Manager), to install these font types for you. Not any more. Now you can install PostScript fonts exactly the same as TrueType fonts using the Windows font installer, or by dragging-and-dropping them into the Fonts folder just like any TrueType font. YEAH! It's about time!

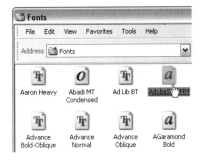

 ## PREVIEW INSTALLED FONTS

If you've owned a computer long enough, I'm sure you've done this at least once. Somehow you got your hands on a disk of 5,000 fonts and, of course, you installed every single one of them. Well, now that you have every font ever created on your computer, it'd be great to know what they actually look like. Here's how to preview your installed fonts.

Click Start>Control Panel, then click Appearance and Themes. Click the Fonts link on the See Also Tasks Pane, then click View on the Fonts folder Menu Bar, and click to check Preview. Now move your pointer over any fonts listed in the window and a quick pre-view of the font pops up. For a larger preview, you can also right-click a font's icon and click Open on the Shortcut menu.

 ASSOCIATE FILES WITH MULTIPLE APPS

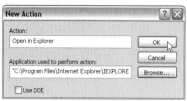

Here's a quick way to associate file types with different programs. Click Start>My Computer>Tools>Folder Options. Click the File Types tab in the dialog box, scroll the Registered File Types, click GIF Image (for example) to highlight it, then click Advanced. Click New in the dialog box, type "Open in Explorer" (without the quotes) in the Action text field. Next, click Browse, navigate to Internet Explorer on your hard drive (usually located at C:\Program Files\Internet Explorer), click Explorer's icon to select it, then click OK. You should now see Open in Explorer listed under Actions. Click OK. Now, right-click any GIF file's icon and you'll have Open in Explorer as an option on the Shortcut menu. Click Open in Explorer to open the file in Explorer instead of its default program.

 "SEND TO" ANYWHERE YOU WANT

A Shortcut menu's Send To menu allows you to send files quickly to popular locations, but you can also customize the Send To menu by adding folders and drives to it—very handy when you frequently send files to the same location. For example, you have a folder named "My Favorite Pics" where you always save, well, your favorite pics. Wouldn't it be convenient to be able to instantly send any picture to this folder by simply using the file's Send To menu?

Here's how: First, make sure you can view hidden files and folders (the Send To folder is hidden by default). Now, right-click Start, click Explore on the Shortcut menu, then Navigate to your Send To folder (usually located at C:\Documents and Settings\Your User Name\SendTo). Simply press-and-hold the Alt key and drag-and-drop the My Favorite Pics folder into the Send To folder to create a shortcut to it. Now, right-click a picture's icon and point to Send To, and click My Favorite Pics to send your pictures instantly to the folder.

FOLDER ICONS?

Have you noticed that folders in Windows Explorer all look alike? This can make it a bit frustrating to find folders quickly. In earlier versions of Windows, there wasn't anything you could do about this; however, this is XP, and you can now change an individual folder's icon. Right-click Start and click Explore on the Shortcut menu. Locate a favorite folder, right-click its icon, and click Properties on the Shortcut menu. Next, click the Customize tab in the dialog box and click Change Icon. Browse your hard drive, select a new icon, and click OK. Then, click OK on the Customize tab. You can now see your folder's new icon. Cool! (*Note*: You may need to launch a new Explorer window to view the changes.)

 HIDDEN APPS—CHAT WITH PEOPLE ON YOUR NETWORK

There's an App named Winchat sitting on your computer right now that lets you chat with users on your network. I use it all the time on both my office and home networks. (I still can't believe it's hidden.) To launch Winchat, click Start and click Run. Type "winchat" (without the quotes) in the Open text field in the dialog box then click OK. This will launch Winchat. Now click Conversation on the Windows Menu Bar and click Dial. Select a computer (available users on the network) to call from the Dial dialog box and click OK. The user's computer will actually ring and invite the user to chat with you. Winchat can usually be located on your hard drive at C:\Windows\System32\winchat. If you have problems locating it, do a search for "winchat" (without the quotes).

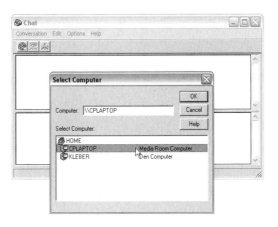

 HIDDEN APPS—CREATE SELF-INSTALLING PACKAGES

With Windows XP and a hidden App named IExpress 2.0, you can actually package your own Apps for installation on other computers. IExpress 2.0 lets you create your own simple self-extracting, self-installing packages of applications. You can even display your custom license agreement before allowing an installation. To launch IExpress 2.0, click Start and click Run. Type "iexpress" (without the quotes) in the Open text field in the dialog box then click OK. Follow the Wizard's step-by-step instructions to create your packages. IExpress 2.0 can usually be located on your hard drive at C:\Windows\System32\iexpress.

 HIDDEN APPS—CUSTOM CHARACTERS

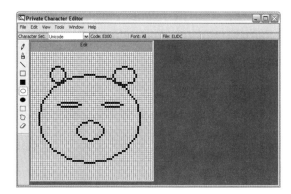

Create your own custom characters with XP's Private Character Editor. Use the Private Character Editor's Draw and Shape tools to turn your name, symbols, or logos into special characters that you can quickly place into your documents using the Windows Character Map. Click Start, then click Run and type "eudcedit" (without the quotes) in the text field in the dialog box. Click OK. This launches Windows Private Character Editor, where you can create and save your own custom characters.

HIDDEN APPS—WHAT HAPPENED TO NETMEETING?

Although NetMeeting has pretty much been replaced by Windows Messenger, I know there are still a lot of you out there who miss the old conferencing program. If you really miss it, you can still use it. NetMeeting is included with XP and just waiting to be installed. To install NetMeeting, click Start, then Run. Type "conf" (without the quotes) in the Open text field in the dialog box, then click OK.

 ## CAPTURE ME IF YOU CAN

You're probably aware that you can take screen captures of your Desktop by pressing the Print Screen (Prt Sc) key on your keyboard, but what do you do if you only want to capture the active window or dialog box? Press-and-hold the Alt key then press the Print Screen key. This keyboard shortcut captures only the active window.

SAVE THAT POP-UP

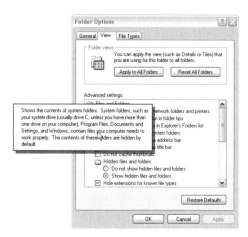

You just used the Help icon to get some info about a task in Windows, and it gave you a pop-up screen with a three-paragraph explanation. This is great, but how in the heck are you supposed to use this? As soon as you click anywhere, the pop-up disappears. The next time this happens to you, copy the explanation and paste it to a text editor, and you'll always have it for reference. To snag a pop-up, press-and-hold the Ctrl key, then press the C key—this copies the text of the Help's explanation. Next, open Notepad and press-and-hold Ctrl-V—this pastes the text into your document. You just saved a pop-up.

 ## OPEN SEVERAL APPS AT ONCE

It's already a little tedious to go to the All Programs menu to launch programs, but when you need to launch several programs for a project, it can be a real chore. For instance, you're creating a new Web site using Dreamweaver, Flash, and Photoshop. You could go to the All Programs menu three different times to launch the three programs, but try this instead. Click Start and point to All Programs. When the menu opens, press-and-hold the Shift key, browse the menu, and click the icons of the programs that you want to open. Each program will launch without closing the All Programs menu.

CREATE A NEW FILE WITHOUT LAUNCHING ITS PROGRAM

How many times have you had a great idea
for the title or description of a document,
only to forget it while spending what seemed
like an hour trying to launch the program
to type your idea and save it? Probably not
as many as I have, but here's a tip that can
help. For example, you can create and name
a new Word Document before you even
launch Word. "What?" you say. Yeah, you can do that, here's
how. Right-click your Desktop, point to New on the Shortcut
menu, and then click Microsoft Word Document. A new Word
document icon will appear on your Desktop ready to be
named. Type the document's title or description and you're
finished. Now, when you're ready, click the icon to launch
Word and edit the document.

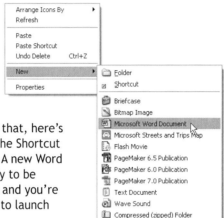

 ## TOP-SECRET, INVISIBLE FOLDERS

Ah, I bet this tip caught your eye! Nothing gets your
attention like top-secret, invisible folders. And you
can make one of those and put it anywhere, even on
your Desktop. First, click Start>My Computer>Folder
Options. Next, click the View tab in the dialog box,
scroll the Advanced settings, click Show Hidden Files
and Folders, then click Apply (keep the dialog box
open). Now, right-click your Desktop, point to New,
and then click Folder on the Shortcut menu. Name
your new folder. Next, right-click the folder's icon
and click Properties on the Shortcut menu. Click the
General tab in the dialog box, check Hidden under
Attributes, then click OK. Now, move into the folder
the files that you want to keep secret. Go back to
the View dialog box, click Do Not Show Hidden Files
and Folders, then Apply. Your folder's now hidden.
Just apply Show/Do Not Show Hidden Files and Folders
to play "Now you see me, now you don't."

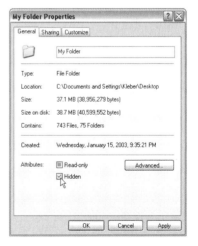

 DO YOU HAVE THE CORRECT TIME?

Synchronize your computer's clock with an Internet time server and you'll always have the correct time. Double-click the time in the Taskbar's notification area, and click the Internet Time tab in the dialog box, then check Automatically Synchronize with an Internet Time Server. Select a server from the drop-down menu and click OK. Now every time you connect to the Internet, your computer's clock will automatically be updated.

 LITTLE HELP PLEASE

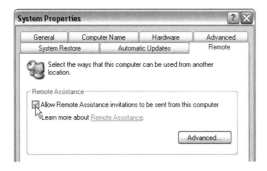

You're having a problem with your computer and you have no idea how to fix it. This isn't so bad because I bet you know someone who does. Why not invite them to help? Using XP's Remote Assistance actually makes it fun to get help from friends. Before you can send an invitation, you have to enable Remote Assistance on your computer: Click Start>My Computer, then click the View System Information link in the System Tasks

Pane. Next, click the Remote tab, check Allow Remote Assistance Invitations to Be Sent from This Computer, then click OK. Now you're able to send invitations for assistance from Outlook, Outlook Express, and Windows Messenger. While using Remote Assistance, your friend will be able to view your computer screen and chat with you in real time. If you allow it, your friends can even use their mouse and keyboard to work with you on your computer. Both you and your friend must be connected to the Internet and running XP to use Remote Assistance.

SEE CLEARLY WITH CLEARTYPE

Laptops should come with pop-up menus
that remind you to blink every once in a
while. There's just something about staring at an LCD screen for hours that feels
like you rubbed your eyes with Q-Tips
dipped in hot wing sauce (don't try this).
You can ease this torture, however, by
enabling ClearType, which can dramatically smooth screen fonts and make type
easier to read.

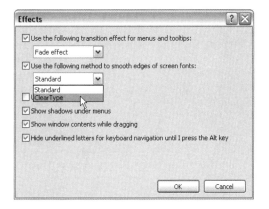

To enable ClearType, right-click the
Desktop and click Properties on the
Shortcut menu. Next, click the Appear-
ance tab in the dialog box and click
Effects. Now, check Use the Following Method to Smooth Edges of Screen Fonts, select
ClearType from the drop-down menu, and then click OK.

SUPER-FAST MEDIA PREVIEWS

Windows Media Player is a fantastic App; however, it's a little overkill when you just want a
quick preview of a media file (video or music).
You can add a preview feature to your media file
types so that you don't have to launch a full-
blown Media Player to view them. Here's how:
Click Start>My Computer>Tools>Folder Options,
then click the File Types tab in the dialog box,
and scroll the Registered file types. Click to highlight MPEG (for
example), then click Advanced in the dialog box. Click New, type
"Preview" (without the quotes) in the Action text box, and type
"C:\Windows\System32\Mplay32.exe" (without the quotes) in the
Application Used to Perform Action text box, then click OK. You
should now see Preview listed under Action. Click OK, then Close
to exit the dialog box. Right-click any MPEG file's icon and you
now have Preview as an option on the Shortcut menu. Click
Preview to quickly launch a mini-player. Much faster!

 SAVE STREAMING MEDIA

Streaming media on the Internet is great, but you can't save it. Right? Actually you can. Once the streaming media has played completely, do a search of your hard drive for the media type played (.AVI, .MPG, .MP3, .WMV, etc.). Here's the trick, however: Make certain when you perform your search that you click the More Advanced Options Pane and check Search Hidden Files and Folders. Once you've finished your search, right-click each file, click Properties on the Shortcut menu, and look at the file's Location to see the referring URL. This helps you to identify the correct file. Now right-click the file, click Copy on the Shortcut menu, then right-click the Desktop, and click Paste. You just saved streaming media.

 KEEP 'EM OUT OF YOUR FOLDERS

There are a couple of ways to keep other users on the computer from viewing your files. First, you can make every folder under your User Profile private (My Documents and its subfolders, Desktop, Start Menu, and Favorites). This means that only you can access these folders and their contents. Other users who try to open your User folder on the hard drive will be denied access.

To do this, right-click Start and click Explore on the Shortcut menu. Right-click your User folder's icon in the Folders Pane and click Properties on the Shortcut menu. Next, click the Sharing tab in the dialog box, check Make This Folder Private, and then click OK. Now all folders and files under your User account are private. If you don't need this much privacy, you don't have to protect your entire User account. You can simply follow the same steps above to make individual folders private instead.

 ## PRINT PHOTO SHEETS

I take a ton of digital photos and absolutely love the picture-printing features in XP. You can print photo sheets of any picture you'd like. Open the folder containing your pictures and click the Print Pictures link on the Picture Tasks Pane. This opens the Photo Printing Wizard.

Just follow the Wizard's instructions to select the pictures you want to print and the layout for your photo sheet. Click Finished when you're through. Now you're printing your own photo sheets.

 ## ORDER PRINTS ONLINE

Don't have a photo printer? Don't sweat it; you can use XP's online print-order feature to send your digital pictures for printing. Here's how. Open the folder containing your pictures and click the Order Prints Online link on the Picture Tasks Pane. This opens the Online Print Ordering Wizard. Just follow the Wizard's instructions to select the pictures you want printed and the online service to use. There are several companies

to choose from, but they all do exactly the same thing. Next, select the pictures' print sizes and quantities. Continue following the Wizard's setup instructions to upload your pictures and provide billing and shipping info.

 TOGGLE DISPLAY OF FILE NAMES IN FILMSTRIP/THUMBNAILS VIEW

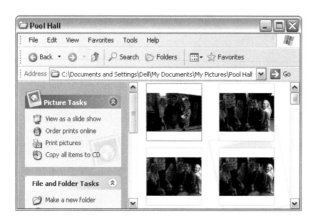

If you're viewing pictures using the Filmstrip or Thumbnails view, there's really no reason to view the file names also. You can already see the picture—the file's name is just taking up valuable space. You can turn file names on and off by pressing the Shift key when you open a folder or when you change to Filmstrip/Thumbnails view using the Views button.

 DRAG-AND-DROP PREVIEWS

If you have pictures saved on your Desktop, you can drag-and-drop them onto an open folder using Filmstrip view to quickly preview them. This doesn't move or copy the pictures; it only displays them for preview.

DISGUISE YOUR FILES

Here's something I bet you didn't know. When saving a file in Notepad or WordPad, if you enclose its name with quotes (e.g. "my file"), the file will be saved without an extension. This means that Windows can't tell what type of file it is and you won't be able to open it. Weird huh? Of course, you'll be able to select an application to try to open it.

Anyway, I'm not exactly certain why anyone would want to use this tip, unless of course you're just a devious person who wants to prevent people from reading your files. But hey, I guess if you're that kind of person, you'll really like this tip.

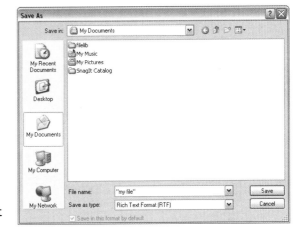

my file

Play That Funky Music

WINDOWS MEDIA
PLAYER 9 TIPS

"They were dancin' and singin'
And movin' to the groovin'
And just when it hit me
Somebody turned around and

Play That Funky Music
windows media player 9 tips

shouted Play that funky music white boy
Play that funky music right . . . "

Isn't this a great song? I love it. I think I was five when it came out, but even then I knew good music. What could be better than a bunch of guys playing R&B Pop? Nothing that I'm aware of. I think Windows Media Player ranks third in the order of Microsoft "killer" Apps. You've got Internet Explorer for browsing the Web, Word for text editing, and then Media Player for pure entertainment—and it just gets better with Media Player 9. If you don't have version 9, then go to Microsoft.com and download it (free), because you'll definitely want it after reading this chapter. Hey, then you can join me and . . . .

"Play that funky music white boy
Lay down the boogie
And play that funky music till you die
Till you die, till you die, till you die . . . . "
   —"Play That Funky Music" by Wild Cherry

 ### SKIN DEEP

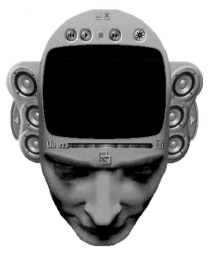

Windows Media Player is shockingly large. I guess it has to be because it does practically everything; but you can change it to Skin mode, which gives you a much smaller and friendlier player. Press Ctrl-2 to switch to Skin mode. Press Ctrl-1 to switch back to Full mode.

 ### SHED YOUR SKIN

Let's shed some skin and change the look of Windows Media Player. Click Skin Chooser on the Taskbar and scroll through the available Skins. Select a new Skin that's just right for you and click Apply Skin. There ya go, a brand-new look!

LOVE THAT SKIN

There's not much point to spending hours looking for the perfect skin if you can't see it when other windows are open. You can keep your player handy by always leaving it on top of open windows. Click Tools>Options, then click the Player tab. Next, check Display on Top When in Skin Mode in the dialog box, and click OK.

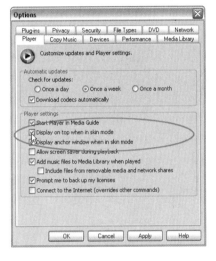

 ANCHORS AWAY

For some reason, Media Player leaves what it calls an Anchor open on your Desktop whenever you minimize your player and you're in Skin mode. What's an Anchor? This thing doesn't even make sense. The Anchor's about as big as the player itself and is really annoying. Here's how to get rid of it: Click Tools>Options, and then click the Player tab. Now, uncheck Display Anchor Window When in Skin Mode, and click OK.

 GET FUNKY

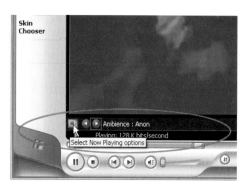

Your music just isn't music until you turn on the funk. Media Player comes with very cool visualizations. Heck, they're the best thing about Media Player. Here's how to turn 'em on. With your music playing, click Now Playing on the Taskbar, click the Now Playing Options button, point to Visualizations, and select the one for you. Feeling groovy? I know you are. To quickly change to a different effect, click the Next Visualization arrow button.

 MAXIMIZE THE FUNK

Okay, it's time to get really "trippy" and take the Visualizations full screen: Double-click anywhere on the Visualizations Pane to maximize the window. (My two-year old daughter and I could stare at it for hours.) Click again to get out of full-screen mode.

I NEED MORE

I know how you feel. You can never have too many effects that zone you out, so let's get more. Click the Now Playing Options button, point to Visualizations, and click Download Visualizations. This will launch your browser and take you to Microsoft's Media Player site, where you can download the latest and greatest.

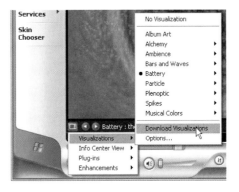

DRAG, DROP, PLAY

You don't have to be in Media Player to open a song. You can play any music file on your computer that's associated to Media Player by right-clicking its icon and clicking Play on its Shortcut menu. Also, you can play a song that's not listed in the Media Library: Just drag-and-drop the music file's icon onto Media Player to play it instantly.

 ## CUSTOM COLOR

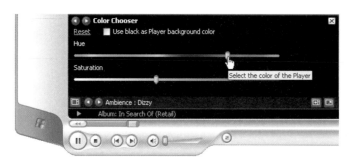

Media Player is so customizable that it even lets you create your own custom colors for it. Here's how: Click the Now Playing Options button, point to Enhancements, and click Color Chooser. Now, just get as weird as you want. Drag the Hue and Saturation sliders to colorize your player. If things get a little too weird, click the Reset link to get back the default colors. You can also choose preset colors by clicking the Change Player Color button.

 ## ALVIN? IS THAT ALVIN?

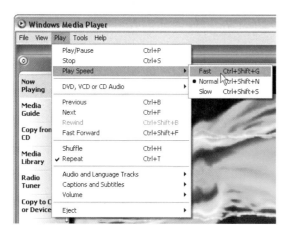

Do you remember when you were a kid playing records and you'd speed up the album to make it sound like Alvin from Alvin and the Chipmunks? Of course you do. We all did it. Unless, of course you're twelve and reading this book, then you have absolutely no idea what I'm writing about. If that's the case, please just move on to the next tip—you're not going to appreciate this. For everyone else, Media Player's brought back the fun. Press Ctrl-Shift-G on your keyboard to fast-play your music, or Ctrl-Shift-S to slow down your music for that Barry White sound. To get back to normal, press Ctrl-Shift-N.

PLAY IT EVEN FASTER

If you really want to kick it into high gear, click the Fast Play button on the Seek Bar. Keep clicking it for speeds up to five times faster than normal. I have no idea what this is good for, but for some reason I just can't leave it alone.

WHAT'S YOUR EQ?

Media Player comes with 21 equalizer presets, and none of them works for me. Go figure. Anyway, you can create your own custom preset by adjusting the equalizer sliders to any setting that you want. Media Player will automatically save your configuration as Custom (found under Now Playing Options>Graphic Equalizer>Custom).

 SUPER-FAST PLAYLISTS

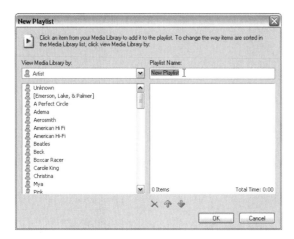

To create a new Playlist quickly, go to your Media Library and click the category heading where you want to create your new Playlist, and then press Ctrl-N. This opens the New Playlist dialog box where you can name your new Playlist and add music files.

 SHORTCUT TO PLAYLISTS

You don't have to go to the Media Library to access your Playlists, just right-click anywhere on the player's controls to get the Quick Access Panel. At the Quick Access Panel, click a Playlist to open it.

ADD FROM ANYWHERE

Here are a couple of quick ways to add media to your Playlists—as you know, you really can never have too many quick ways to add media to your Playlists. Just right-click any media file anywhere on your computer and click Add to Playlist on the Shortcut menu. This opens the My Playlists dialog box where you select a Playlist or create a new one. You can also drag-and-drop files to Playlists in Media Library.

 ### ADD 'EM ALL AT ONCE

If you have a folder of media files to add to a Playlist, you don't have to add each file separately. Simply right-click the folder and click Add to Playlist on the Shortcut menu. Now, select a Playlist or create a new one using the dialog box, then click OK and all of the files in the folder will be added instantly.

 IT'S AUTOMATIC

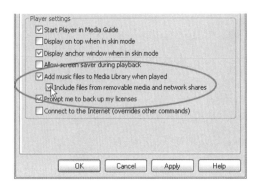

Here's a tip that can make your life a little easier. You can add music automatically to Media Library when it's played: Click Tools>Options, then click the Player tab. Now, check the box to Add Music Files to Media Library When Played. Check Include Files from Removable Media and Network Shares to add files played from these locations as well.

 GIVE IT ONE STAR

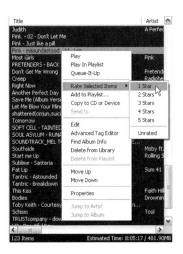

If you've ever accidentally downloaded a really bad song—you know, you thought you were downloading Blink 182 but what you got was A Flock of Seagulls—don't just delete the fraudulent file, humiliate it. Give it a one-star rating. Media Player lets you rate your media files from one to five stars.

To rate your music, right-click the file's name, point to Rate Selected Items on the Shortcut menu, and then click a rating. Now, give the Flock a shameful one-star rating. Go ahead, it'll make you feel better. I figure that one-star rating's got to be used for something.

BUILT-IN POWER SORTING

If you're not using Media
Player's Auto Playlists, you
should be. All music located in
the Media Library is automatically sorted by Auto Playlists.
Let's say you want to listen to
all of the music that you've
rated 4 or 5 stars. Well, click Go
to the Media Library, then Auto
Playlist, and there's a 4- and
5-star-rated Playlist already set
up and ready to play or copy
to disk.

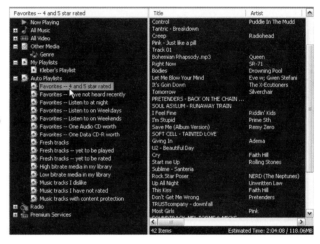

 LET'S SORT IT OUT

Another way to sort your music is by clicking
the column headers of a Playlist. You can add
more columns by right-clicking any header in
the Media Library and selecting new columns
on the menu. When you're finished adding
columns, rearrange them by dragging-and-
dropping them in any order you want in the
Media Library.

 SURPRISE ME

Want to mix things up a bit? Click the Shuffle button to, well, shuffle the play order of your Playlist. Click the button again to return the Playlist to its original order. You can also press Ctrl-H to shuffle your Playlist quickly.

 QUEUE-IT-UP

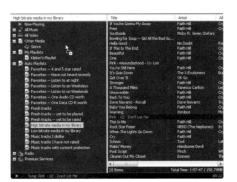

If you want to just listen to a music file without adding it to your Media Library, you can "Queue-It-Up." Right-click a media file anywhere on your computer and click Queue-It-Up on the Shortcut menu or drag-and-drop the file onto the Playlist Pane in Now Playing.

IT'S MINI-PLAYER!

Yeah! I love mini-player! A new feature
of Media Player 9 is the mini-player. I
use it constantly: It's got everything and
it's always visible on the Windows Taskbar for easy access. To use mini-player,
right-click the Windows Taskbar, point
to Toolbars on the Shortcut menu, then
click Windows Media Player. You must
have Media Player 9 installed to see this
option. Now, when you minimize Media Player,
it becomes mini-player on the Taskbar.

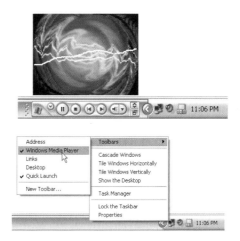

MINI-PLAYER'S MINI INFO

Want to know what song is playing when
you're using mini-player? You don't have to
restore Media Player: Just scroll over the
Windows logo on the mini-player and the Info
Pane pops up showing the file's info.

 MINI-FUNK

Mini-player's cool: It's not just Media Player without the funk—and Microsoft knew this. So, mini-player comes complete with Mini-Visualizations. Click the Show Video and Visualization Window button to display the effects. You can quickly change effects by clicking the window. Click the button again to turn off the window.

 PLAY IT AGAIN

Just can't get enough of that song? Well, the fun never has to stop. Press Ctrl-T when a song or Playlist is playing and it will continuously repeat.

IT'S A CONTROL THING

The one thing you'll probably find yourself doing more than anything else in Media Player is adjusting the volume—up, down, or off. The quickest way to do this is to use the keyboard. Here are a few keyboard shortcuts to help you out: Press F10 to pump up the volume, F9 to turn it down, and F8 to mute it.

 IT'S WORTH WAITING FOR

If you're using a standard modem (56 Kb) to connect to the Internet, then you're probably used to streaming media pausing, stopping, and then restarting. This kind of defeats the purpose of streaming media, doesn't it? Well, maybe you can't do anything about your connection, but you can do something about the poor streaming media.

Increase the amount of time your player spends buffering the stream and you'll get a much better stream, free of breaks and pauses. Click Tools>Options, then click the Performance tab, and increase your Network Buffering. By default, buffering is set to 5 seconds. You can increase the Buffer up to 60 seconds of content. Increase it as much as necessary to get media to stream properly.

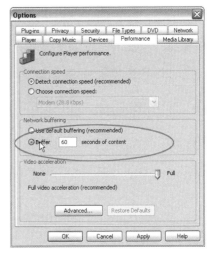

 MAKE IT RIGHT

Often when you download music from the Web, the song or group's name will be misspelled or it might list the wrong genre. Well, you can quickly change a song's info using the Advanced Tag Editor. Right-click a song title and click Advanced Tag Editor on the Shortcut menu. On the Track Info tab, you can change whatever info needs correcting, or you can add new info to help you to identify and sort the file.

 GETTIN' GEEKY

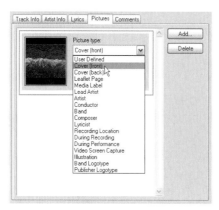

Okay, it's time to get really geeky with Media Player. If you don't like an album's cover art, you can change it to anything you'd like. Here's how: Right-click any song title and click Advanced Tag Editor on the Shortcut menu. Next, click the Pictures tab in the dialog box and click Add to browse your hard drive to locate the image you want to use. Now, select a Picture Type—this is what you'd like your photo to represent, which can be anything from the album's cover to the band picture. Click Apply, and you're done.

I'LL TELL YOU WHERE TO LOOK

Media Player automatically monitors your My Music folder for changes and updates the Media Library whenever new files are added to it. Which is fine, but you're a rebel. You save your music to a different folder on your hard drive. So, how can you make Media Player monitor this folder also? Please send $5.00 and a stamped return address envelope to... just kidding.

Click Tools>Options, then click the Media Library tab in the dialog box, and click Monitor Folders. Now, click Add to select the folder(s) on your hard drive that you want Media Player to monitor. You can also remove locations from here, including the default My Music folder.

CAN'T TAKE THE HIGHS AND LOWS

Okay, I've done my fair share of downloading music from the Web, and I'm sure you probably have too. You've probably noticed that there can be a huge difference in the quality of music you download. The biggest problem is with the volume level from song to song, and it can be a real pain to constantly adjust the player's volume. Well, there's a way to fix this problem: Turn on Auto Volume Leveling.

From Now Playing, click the Now Playing Options button, point to Enhancements, and click Crossfading and Auto Volume Leveling. Next, click the Turn on Auto Volume Leveling link. Now all the music in the Playlist will sound the same.

 ## LEVEL THE PLAYING FIELD

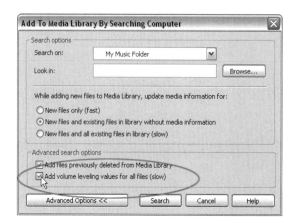

Save yourself the hassle of turning on Volume Leveling for each Playlist; instead, level your tracks when they're first imported into the Media Library. Here's how: Click File on the Menu Bar, point to Add to Media Library, and then click By Searching Computer. Next, click Browse to select the folder containing the Windows Media or MP3 files to which you want to add Volume Leveling. Now, click Advanced Options and check Add Volume Leveling Values for All Files (Slow). Media Player will now automatically add Volume Leveling to the files as they're added to the Media Library.

 ## CAN YOU RELATE?

Has this ever happened to you? You come across a song that you love. It's perfect for the moment, event, whatever, and you'd love to find similar music but don't know where to start looking. This actually happens to me a lot. Kind of sad isn't it? Well, Media Player can help.

When you have a song playing and the Info Center view is open, click the Related Music link. Wasn't so obvious until I pointed it out, was it? Anyway, clicking this link will automatically search the Web and return a list of similar (related) music. Very cool! If you don't see the Info Center view, you can open it by going to Now Playing and clicking View on the Menu Bar, then clicking Info Center View>Always Show.

SING ALONG

Did you know that you could add your own lyrics to your favorite songs? You can. Click the Lyrics button in the Info Center view and then click Add Lyrics. Now you can type or paste in the lyrics for the song. Click Save Lyrics when you're finished.

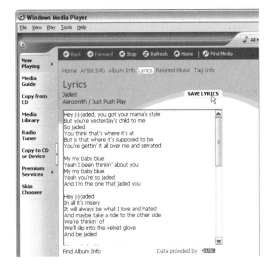

 WOW!

The SRS WOW Effect is the best new enhancement in Media Player 9—it blew me away. The WOW effect simulates Surround Sound for small or large speakers, or even headphones. It works wonders on my laptop speakers. To WOW your computer speakers, click the Now Playing Options button on the Info Center view, point to Enhancements, and click SRS WOW Effects. Next, click the Turn On link. Now, throw in your favorite DVD or play a music file and check out the difference!

 YOU CAN FIND IT FROM HERE

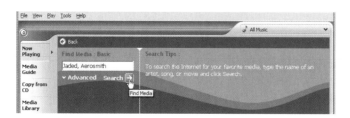

Media Player is not only a great tool for playing music, it's also fantastic for searching for media. From the Info Center view, click Find Media. Type the name of a band, song, or album, and click Search. The results page displays all media found—music and video. Pretty cool!

 IT'S ALL IN THE NAME

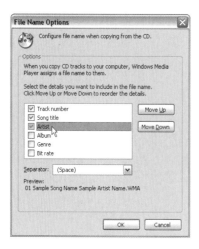

Follow this one closely. It can get a little confusing. By default, when you copy music from a CD, Media Player names your tracks using the track number and song title, which is good. It's nice to know the name of your music, but you can automatically add details to the song's name when it's saved. You can add the artist's name, album, genre, and bit rate. So, a title that would usually look like "01_Jaded" could look like "01_Jaded_Aerosmith_Rock." This is really handy for identifying and sorting your music. Here's how to do it.

Click Tools>Options, then click the Copy Music tab in the dialog box, and click File Name. Now, check the details that you want to add to the file name. You can also change the order of the details and add different types of separators.

THIS ISN'T GOING ANYWHERE

I have no idea why Media Player automatically starts up in Media Guide. This is a real pain if you're not connected to the Internet, because Media Player will spend several seconds looking for a connection. This is a good five seconds of torture. I know it's not going anywhere. Well, you can spare yourself this torment and turn off Media Guide at startup. Click Tools>Options, then click the Player tab in the dialog box. Next, uncheck Start Player in Media Guide, then click OK. Now when you launch Media Player, it opens to Now Playing.

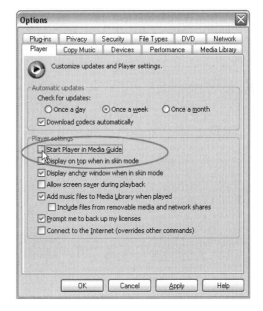

It's a
Small World

INTERNET EXPLORER TIPS

There's no doubt that the Internet is the greatest technology of my generation, that and the Xbox© of course,

It's a Small World

explore your world with internet explorer

and it's now the number one reason for owning a personal computer, though some would say it's not all good. The Net's made us gleefully lazy. It's true; I have no reason ever to leave my house. I bet there's someone sitting in a burning house right now just waiting for his computer to save him (or her). I wonder what Lewis and Clark would think of this new tool of exploration—probably not much. They'd probably whack all of us in the head. Chill out Lewis and Clark—that's exactly what makes the Internet great. We don't have to be Lewis or Clark to examine the buffalo-hunting tribes that lived along the Missouri. We can just fire up our computers. Lazy? Sure. Putting the world literally at our fingertips? Absolutely—explore away!

 DON'T TYPE YOUR URLS

Let's see—http://www. That's not right; let's try again: http://www.disnee.com. No, that's not right either. Why can't I do this? Why is this so hard? It's not our fault. Typing http://www.yada-yada-yada.blah just isn't natural. It just feels wrong, so don't do it. In Internet Explorer's Address Bar simply type the site's domain name (e.g. Disney), then press-and-hold Ctrl and hit Enter. This keyboard shortcut wraps "http://www." and ".com" stuff around the domain name you typed and launches the URL. And, if your site doesn't use .com, don't sweat it. Internet Explorer keeps searching for the site using various extensions.

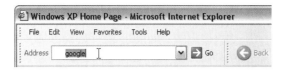

 BACK AND FORTH IN A FLASH

You probably know that you can use the back and forward buttons to go backward or forward exactly one page; however if you want to jump several pages at once, click the Down Arrow beside the buttons to view recently visited pages. Click on any page title to jump to it immediately.

BACK AND FORTH USING THE KEYBOARD

Another quick way to move back and forth is to use your keyboard. Press the Alt key then the Left and Right Arrow keys to jump backward and forward, respectively, through recently visited pages.

YOU SHOULD KNOW YOUR HISTORY

Okay, you're browsing the Web and you come across the coolest site you've ever seen, and right at that moment your browser crashes. You didn't have time to Bookmark the site and you can't remember how you got there. Well, you're just out of luck; you'll never find that site again—just kidding. You can actually view every site you've visited in the last couple of weeks. Yeah, isn't that great? Internet Explorer automatically saves where you've been on the Web. To check out where you've been surfin', click the History button to open the History Pane. Now, you can search for sites you visited today, yesterday, or two weeks ago.

 QUICK FAVORITES

Here's a handy Favorites tip. Press Ctrl-D on your keyboard to quickly add the current Web page to your Favorites folder.

 DRAG-AND-DROP FAVORITES

The previous tip works great for quickly adding Web pages to Favorites, but it doesn't let you specify a folder within Favorites—which makes it fast, but not friendly. And using the Add to Favorites dialog box is, well, clunky. There's a better way. Click the Favorites button to display the Favorites Pane. Now, you can simply drag-and-drop URLs from the Address Bar to any folder within Favorites.

THAT MAKES NO SENSE

You know, I think there's a conspiracy out there to name Web pages as vaguely as possible. Half the time a page's title has nothing to do with the actual content of the page. This can make it almost impossible to locate the page in Favorites later. You can prevent this by renaming saved Favorites to something more descriptive that will help you to remember what the page is all about. Right-click the title of a Favorite and click Rename on the Shortcut menu. Now, simply type any name you want.

 FOLDERS FOR FAVORITES

Eventually you're going to need to add new folders to Favorites to help keep things organized. Here's how to do it fast: Right-click anywhere in the Folders Pane and click Create New Folder on the Shortcut menu. A new folder appears ready to be named. You just created a new Favorites folder.

 NEVER ORGANIZE FAVORITES

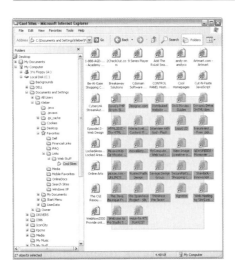

Never—I repeat never—use the Organize Favorites dialog box to organize Favorites. It hates you. Well, it probably doesn't actually hate you, but the way it works, you definitely wouldn't call it your friend. There's a much better way to organize Favorites. Click Favorites on the Menu Bar, then press-and-hold the Shift key and click Organize Favorites. This opens Favorites in its own window; now you can select any number of pages and move them anywhere you'd like. Grab multiple folders and drag them to other folders. Select multiple pages and delete them. Just go nuts. By the way, for whatever tortuous reason, you can't do this using the Organize Favorites dialog box. There, you can only move or delete a single page or folder at a time.

 HOME'S A DRAG

To set Internet Explorer's home page quickly, click the page's icon in the Address Bar and drag-and-drop it onto the Home button. This shortcut instantly sets the page you're viewing as your browser's home page.

SPEED SEARCH

You don't have to open the Search Pane to search the Web in Explorer. Instead, try typing your keywords or question directly in the Address Bar, and then click Go. Explorer will search the Web and display the results.

 I WANT A NEW WINDOW

Don't we all? You can never have too many new Explorer windows. In fact, I know exactly how many new Explorer windows I can open before my computer runs out of memory and crashes. It's a lot, but that's not the point. Often, you want to leave your Web page visible, but you also want to continue browsing the Web. What to do? Hmm, let's try pressing Ctrl-N. Hey, that worked: a brand new Explorer window.

 LIKE IT? SEND IT TO A FRIEND

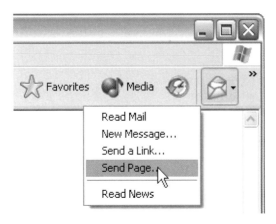

If you come across a Web page that you've just got to tell your friends about, why not do it right then and there? Click the Mail button and click Send Page on the menu. This will automatically open Outlook Express with the page attached. Now, simply type your friend's e-mail address in the To box and click Send.

 DON'T JUST SEND IT; ARCHIVE IT

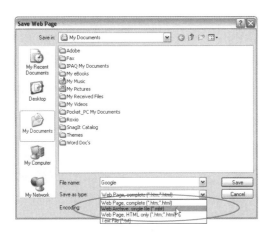

Using the previous tip, your friend can only view the page you sent them if they're online, which is probably fine, after all they had to be online to receive your e-mail, right? True, but you can create a Web archive and save all of the information needed to display the page in a single MIME-encoded file. They won't have to be online to actually open and view the page.

To create an archive of a Web page, click File on the Menu Bar, then click Save As. Choose a location, perhaps your Desktop, to save the file, then in the Save As Type box, select Web Archive, Single File, and click Save. Now attach the file to your e-mail and send it. When your friend opens the file, it will launch her browser and display the page exactly as it appears on the Web.

ERASE YOUR HISTORY

There's gonna come a time when you need to erase your browser's history. Maybe your anniversary is coming up and you've been checking out jewelry Web sites for that perfect gift for your wife. Or, you're planning a romantic getaway with your husband and don't want him to know that you've spent the last two days browsing Travelocity® for the best airfares to the Bahamas. I understand, and I'm here to help you keep your secret. Click Tools>Internet Options. Next, click the General tab in the dialog box and click Clear History. Now you can relax, your secret is safe.

 ## COVER YOUR TRACKS

This tip falls in line with the whole cover-your-tracks idea. Internet Explorer caches the Web sites that you visit to a folder named Temporary Internet Files. Caching helps to make Web sites load faster the next time you visit them. Assuming that you visit the same sites frequently, this is pretty useful. It can also show where you've been surfing—not always a good thing. You can quickly delete these files at any time. Click Tools>Internet Options, then click the General tab in the dialog box. Next, click Delete Files (under Temporary Internet Files), and all cached files are now gone.

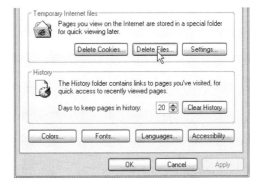

 ## COVER YOUR TRACKS AUTOMATICALLY

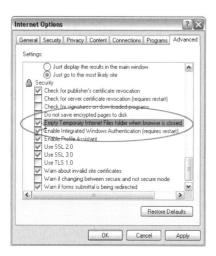

If you're really serious about keeping people out of your browsing business, you can automatically delete your cached files every time you close your browser. To do this, click Tools>Internet Options, and click the Advanced tab in the dialog box. Next, scroll to Security, check Empty Temporary Internet Files Folder When Browser Is Closed, and then click Apply. Now, every time you close your browser, your cached files will automatically be deleted.

 ## MASTER OF DISGUISE

Let's say for whatever reason, you really don't won't to delete your cached Internet files but you still don't want anyone to know where you've been browsing. Well, you can get really clever and move your Temporary Internet Files folder, and here's how: Click Tools>Internet Options, and click Settings on the General tab. Next, click Move Folder, select a new location on your hard drive to save your cached Internet files, and click OK.

Now, if you want to get really freaky about covering your tracks, you can make the folder hidden. Right-click the folder and click Properties on the Shortcut menu. Next, check Hidden on the General tab of the dialog box and then click OK—but, good grief, what in the world are you doing on the Web? Never mind, it's none of my business.

I DON'T NEED THAT MUCH SPACE

For some reason, Internet Explorer reserves
enough of your hard drive to cache probably about one-third of the entire Internet.
Personally, I'd much rather use my disk space
for more important things. You can reduce the
amount of disk space reserved for Internet
Explorer by clicking Tools>Internet Options.
Next, click the General tab in the dialog box
and, under Temporary Internet Files, click
Settings. Now, grab the slider and pull it to the
left to decrease the amount of disk space used
by Explorer. Once you've changed it to a more
reasonable amount, click OK.

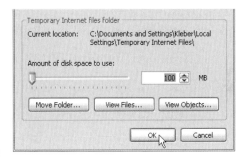

 ## POWER SEARCH

By default, when Explorer searches the Web,
it takes you to the most likely site. But you
can make it take you to the most likely site
and display the search results at the same
time. This gives you tons more options and
ultimately speeds up your searches. Here's
how: Click Tools>Internet Options, and click
the Advanced tab in the dialog box. Next,
scroll the Settings, and under Search from the
Address Bar, check Display Results, and Go to
the Most Likely Site, then click Apply. Now
perform a search and look at the difference.
Much better!

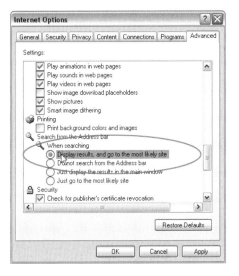

 SUPER-FAST BROWSING

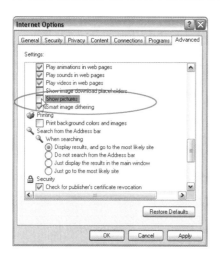

This tip is for people with low-bandwidth connections to the Web. If you're browsing a news site where what's important is the text and not the graphics, then turn 'em off. This can dramatically increase your browsing speed. To turn off graphics, just click Tools>Internet Options, and click the Advanced tab in the dialog box. Next, scroll the Settings, and under Multimedia, uncheck Show Pictures, then click Apply. No more graphics means super-fast browsing.

 VIEW IT OFFLINE

I use this tip all the time. I travel quite a bit, and if you do too, you already know that you can't use wireless devices while in flight. So, browsing the Web just isn't going to happen while you're 30,000 feet in the air. But this doesn't mean that you can't actually view Web pages; you just need to save them for offline viewing.

Navigate to the page you want to be able to view offline, add the page to Favorites, check Make Available Offline, and then click OK. Next right-click the title of the page in Favorites and click Synchronize on the Shortcut menu. Now, just select the page from Favorites when you're working offline to view it.

 TAKE IT A STEP FURTHER

The previous tip showed you how to view a Web page offline, but what if you want more than just the one page? Well, you can do that too. Right-click the Web page in Favorites (that you just made available offline) and click Properties on the Shortcut menu. Next, click the Download tab in the dialog box, type in how many links deep (up to 3) from this page that you'd like to make available offline, and check whether or not to follow links outside of the page's Web site. When finished, click OK. Now, right-click the title of the page in Favorites and click Synchronize on the Shortcut menu.

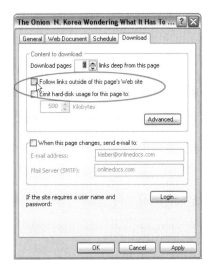

 QUICK SAVE WEB GRAPHICS

You can quickly save just about any graphic (pictures, photos, animations) you see while browsing the Web. Simply right-click the image and click Save Picture As on the Shortcut menu. Now, choose a location on your hard drive where you want to save it and click Save. You can do this even faster by simply dragging-and-dropping an image from Explorer onto your Desktop.

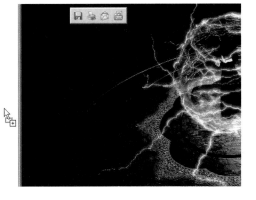

 MAKE IT YOUR BACKGROUND

Maybe simply saving that Web graphic isn't good enough? You love it so much you've just got to see it all the time. That's okay, it's happened to me too. Well, you can set any image displayed in your browser as your Desktop's background: Just right-click the image and click Set as Background on the Shortcut menu. Now you can see it all the time, any time.

 CLEARING PASSWORDS

When you're looking for files in either List view or Column view, it's almost certain that by default, Internet Explorer's AutoComplete feature will save passwords, addresses, and other information entered into forms. This means you don't have to re-enter the information each time you visit a site. That's good, but—it also means that someone using your computer can access your password-protected accounts. That's not good. So, there may be times when it's necessary to clear your passwords, and here's how: Click Tools>Internet Options, then click the Content tab in the dialog box. Next, click AutoComplete Settings, uncheck Usernames and Passwords on Forms, and then click OK.

WHO'S RELATED?

There's a button available on the Standard Buttons Toolbar
labeled Related that should really be on the Toolbar by default—
but it's not. It's my favorite button. Well, that and the Refresh
button. I just can't get enough of Refresh, can you? Anyway,
Related (Powered by Alexa) will find sites similar to the one
you're currently viewing. This can make hunting down info on the
Web much easier. To add the Related button, right-click the Standard Buttons Toolbar and click Customize on the Shortcut menu.
Scroll the Available Toolbar buttons, click Related, and then click
Add. Now, browse to a favorite site and click Related.
Note: If Related isn't listed on your Available Toolbar button
menu, then visit Alexa.com to get it.

SMART PRINTING

I have to admit it—I'm a sports nut. I practically
live on ESPN's Web site. When I find a topic of
interest, such as the Tampa Bay Buccaneers
(they rule!), I'll read the article and just about
every related link on the page. I'll even print
articles to take with me to read later. Well,
I discovered a way to get really geeky and print
not only the page I'm viewing, but all of the
associated pages that are linked to it as well. If
you want to get geeky like me, try this: First,

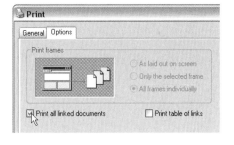

put a ream of paper in your printer, click File>Print, then click the Options tab in the
dialog box. Next, check Print All Linked Documents, and click Print.

YOU DON'T HAVE TO SEE IT TO SAVE IT

This tip works best for saving media. More often than not when you click a video or audio link, the media will stream in your browser, and it doesn't give you the option to save it to your hard drive. Well, if you decide you want to save the media, right-click the referring link and click Save Target As on the Shortcut menu. This allows you to download the file and save it to wherever you'd like.

SEND IT TO YOUR DESKTOP

If you want to save a Web page displayed in your browser, you can right-click anywhere on the page and click Create Shortcut to send it to your Desktop. Or you can simply click the URL's icon in the Address Bar and drag-and-drop it onto your Desktop.

TAB YOUR WAY THROUGH FORMS

Online forms are a pain. They're necessary and useful but not a whole lot of fun to navigate. Clicking your mouse in each text box to type in them just seems, I don't know, painful. Let's stop the insanity and use the Tab key on the keyboard to navigate forms. Press the Tab key to jump from field to field. Press Shift-Tab to jump back to previous fields.

 ## ONE-CLICK FAVORITES

In earlier chapters, I wrote about the power of the Links Toolbar, and since the Links Toolbar was actually intended for Internet Explorer, I guess it would be appropriate to mention it in this chapter as well. You probably know where this is going.

The Links Toolbar is the perfect place to hold your most important and frequently visited sites. To place a Web page on the Links Toolbar, simply click the URL's icon in the Address Bar and drag-and-drop it onto the Links Toolbar. Now your favorite links are always visible—just one click away. To show your Links Toolbar, right-click the Standard Buttons Toolbar and click Links on the Shortcut menu.

Come Together

E-MAIL MADE EASY

You know, e-mail is exactly what I needed in my life. I'm a maniac! I need to do everything faster and better. It's just the way I am.

Come Together

e-mail made easy

And, being able to communicate faster and better is right up my alley. Honestly, I can't even remember my professional life without e-mail. How did you old guys get along without it? Geez, I bet you actually owned a typewriter. You must be so old, your memory is in black and white. Yep, you're so old, you walked into an antique store and they kept you. I'm sorry. I have no excuse. I just had another birthday and it makes me feel better to berate anyone older. I'm not handling it well. With that said, the key on Benjamin Franklin's kite was to your house. I'm sorry. I can't stop. Please, just turn the page.

 I JUST WANT TO START UP

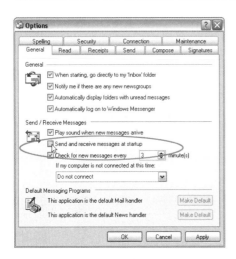

I'm not sure why Send and Receive Messages at Startup is set up as the default. I personally think this is the most annoying thing since "The Thong Song." I mean, sometimes I just want to open Outlook Express and type an e-mail, read an e-mail, or just look at my e-mail. Unfortunately, there's not a kill option for this feature, only Off. Here's how to do it. Click Tools>Options, then click the General tab, and uncheck Send and Receive Messages at Startup. Click OK. Whew, that's better!

 YOU'VE GOT A NEW MAIL SOUND

By default Outlook Express uses the Windows XP Notification, which sounds kind of like every other XP sound. So, if you'd actually like to know that you've received new e-mail, you can make the notification sound a little more distinguishable. Click Start>Control Panel>Sound, Speech, and Audio Devices>Sounds and Audio Devices, then click the Sounds tab in the dialog box, scroll to find then select New Mail Notification in Program Events. Now, choose a new sound from the Sounds drop-down menu or browse your hard drive to choose a new sound. If you have AOL installed on your computer, you may want to use AOL's "You've Got Mail" sound. When you're finished, click OK.

GO DIRECTLY TO YOUR INBOX

When launching Outlook Express, I always go to my Inbox first, typically because I'm opening the program to check for new e-mail and it just saves time to start there. To take the fast track to your Inbox, click Tools>Options, then click the General tab in the dialog box. Next, check When Starting, Go Directly to My 'Inbox' Folder, then click OK. Now Outlook Express will open in your Inbox.

 READ IT, BUT LEAVE IT

It's pretty convenient to be able to check your e-mail on the road using your laptop, PDA, or from another computer, but what's not convenient is that the mail is then removed from your server: By default, incoming messages are automatically deleted from your server when received. So, what do you do to be able to read the received mail from other computers? Leave copies of your e-mail on the server, which allows you to download it again later from another location.

Here's how: Click Tools>Accounts and click the Mail tab in the dialog box. Next, click to highlight the e-mail account that you're checking for new messages and then click Properties. Now, click the Advanced tab and check Leave a Copy of Messages on Server, and click OK. You'll now be able to download the same messages from different computers.

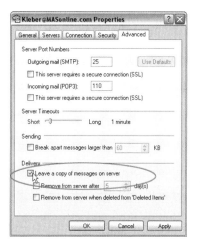

 GROUP 'EM

 If you often e-mail the same message to several people—for instance, family, friends, or co-workers—you should create a group. Groups make it much easier to send multiple contacts the same message at the same time. To create a group, click the Address Book button, then click New in your Address Book, and select New Group. This opens the New Group Properties dialog box where you can name the group and select members from your existing contacts. When finished, click OK. Your new group's name now appears in your Contacts. To send e-mail to the group, simply type or select the group's name in the To field. Now everyone in the group will be sent the message.

 ADD NEW MEMBERS

 This isn't as obvious as you might think. To add contacts to an existing group, click the Address Book button on the Toolbar to open your Address Book. Next, scroll your Contacts, locate the group where you want to add new members, and double-click the group's name to open it. Now, use the dialog box to add new members, remove existing members, or create new contacts for the group. Click OK once you're finished.

BCC IS BETTER

Something to keep in mind when sending
e-mail to groups is that everyone receiving
the message will see the e-mail address
for each member on the list—some people
in the group may not be crazy about this.
There's a clever way around this problem,
however. On a new message window, click
To to select the recipients, but instead of
adding your group to the To field, add it
to the Bcc (Blind Carbon Copy) field. Now
when you send messages to the group,
members will only see who sent the message, not who the recipients were.

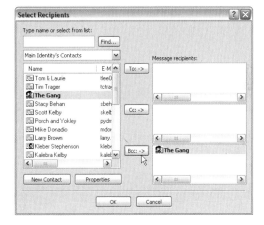

 RIGHT-CLICK TO E-MAIL

To quickly send e-mail to contacts, try right-clicking
their names in Contacts and clicking Send E-Mail on
the Shortcut menu. If you don't see Contacts, click
View>Layout, check Contacts, and then click OK. You'll
now see Contacts beneath the Folder List.

 MANAGE YOUR MAIL

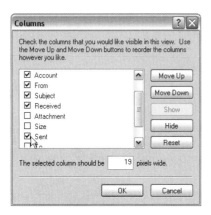

You can organize Outlook Express' Messages Pane the same way as Details in folder views. You can add columns by right-clicking any column header, clicking Columns on the Shortcut menu, and then checking the columns that you want to appear. You can also arrange columns by grabbing any column header and dragging-and-dropping it in any order you'd like.

 WHAT'S THE SUBJECT?

Click on any column header to sort your messages quickly; for example, click Received to list your messages by the date and time they were received or click Subject to sort messages by their subject line. If you have multiple accounts, you might want to sort by using the Accounts column. This will tell you which accounts received messages.

FLAG IT

I receive a ridiculous amount of e-mail throughout the day, and if I'm expecting an important e-mail, I'll set up a message rule to automatically flag it to notify me that it has arrived. To flag incoming messages, click Tools>Message Rules>Mail and create a new mail rule using the dialog box. In the first menu, check Where the From Line Contains People; in the second menu, check Flag It; and in the third menu, click on the Contains link and add the person's name and e-mail address. Next, name your new rule and click OK. Now, when a message arrives from this person, it will be flagged immediately for easy recognition.

 YEP, WE RECEIVED IT

This works best for accounts that receive lots of e-mails with similar requests; for instance, your Web site's Info account. This e-mail account might receive tens or even hundreds of e-mails each day requesting information and it might take you days to respond. To create an auto-reply that lets senders know that you've received their messages, open Notepad by clicking Start>All Programs>Accessories>Notepad, type a generic reply, and save it wherever you'd like using the ".eml" extension (e.g. reply.eml). This saves your reply as an e-mail message.

Now open Outlook Express, click Tools>Message Rules>Mail, and create a new mail rule using the dialog box. In the first menu, check Where the Message Is from the Specified Account; in the second menu, check Reply with Message; and in the third menu, click the Specified link and add the account that receives the messages. Click the Message link, navigate to the reply that you created earlier in Notepad, and select it. Next, name your new rule and click OK. Now, when a message is received by this account, your reply will be sent automatically.

 SHORTCUT TO YOUR BEST FRIEND

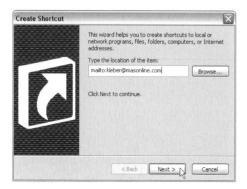

Do you have someone who you e-mail a lot—a friend, family member, or co-worker? Of course you do, so this tip will make your life a bit easier. Right-click your Desktop, point to New, and click Shortcut on the Shortcut menu. In the Type the Location of the Item field, type mailto:*your friend's e-mail address*—for example, mailto: kleber@masonline.com—then click Next. Give your shortcut a name and click Finish. Now, when you click your friend's e-mail shortcut on your Desktop, a new mail message window will open with your friend's e-mail address already in the To field. Just type your message and click Send.

 PERSONAL PHONE BOOK

Here's a quick way to have your Contacts' phone numbers available: Just click the Address Book button and click Print on the Address Book Toolbar. Now, select All for the Print Range, Phone List for the Print Style, and then click Print. This will print a complete list of your Contacts' phone numbers. You can also select Business Card for the Print Style to print each Contact's business card.

SIGN IT AND FORGET IT

For most accounts, especially business accounts, you'll almost always have the same Signature—meaning that you'll usually end your messages with the same name and any contact information. You don't have to type this information each time you send an e-mail (unless you just really like to type). You can create a Signature just once and add it to your messages whenever you want.

Here's how: Click Tools>Options, then click the Signatures tab in the dialog box. Next, click New and give your Signature a name. In the Edit Signature dialog box, select Text, then type your Signature, and click OK. You can also select a text file on your hard drive to use for your signature. To use your new Signature, open a New Message window and place your cursor in the message where you want your signature to appear. Now, click Insert>Signature to place the Signature into your message.

 ## DID YOU GET MY MESSAGE?

Don't you hate not knowing whether someone received your e-mail? I mean, you asked for a reply but, of course, they never sent one. So, you're just left hanging. Did they get it? Did my server eat it? You don't know and because they won't reply, you never will. Stressful, isn't it? Well, there's a way that you can encourage the recipient to acknowledge that they received your e-mail. From a New Message window (before you send your message), click Tools>Request Read Receipt. Now, when they receive your message, they'll be prompted to acknowledge that they received it. If they do, you'll receive notification that it was received. If they don't, then subscribe their e-mail address to every spammer on the Web. That'll teach 'em!

  SNAG THAT STATIONERY

Someone just sent you an e-mail and it has the coolest stationery attached that you've ever seen. Wouldn't it be great if you could snag it for yourself? You're in luck, you can.

With the e-mail message open, displaying the stationery in the Preview Pane, click File>Save as Stationery. Next, name the stationery and click Save. Now, when you apply stationery to messages, you'll see your new stationery listed. Oh, and by the way, be sure to send your friend a thank-you note for using their stationery—they'll appreciate that.

  I CAN'T GET ENOUGH

Yeah, this stationery stuff is great, isn't it? Just can't get enough? Me too, so let's keep the fun rollin' and go nuts downloading all we can get our hands on. Click Tools>Options, then click the Compose tab in the dialog box. Next, click Download More. This opens your browser and takes you to a download page at Microsoft's Web site. Now, select new Stationery and follow the online instructions for installing the downloads.

DO-IT-YOURSELF STATIONERY

If you're familiar with basic HTML, you can
create you own custom Stationery. This is great
for branding corporate e-mail. Using FrontPage,
Dreamweaver, GoLive, or any HTML editor,
create an HTML page using your own graphics and background colors and save it to your
Stationery folder with the extensions ".html"
or ".htm." (The Stationery folder should be
located at C:\Program Files\Common Files\
Microsoft Shared\Stationery. If you have trouble
locating it, do a search for "Stationery.") Next,
simply copy your saved Stationery and any
graphics to the Stationery folder. Now, your
new Stationery is available for e-mail messages.

You can also create a simpler version of custom Stationery using the Stationery Setup
Wizard. Click Tools>Options, then click the Compose tab in the dialog box. Next, click Create
New and follow the Wizard's directions for creating custom Stationery.

 THINGS TO DO

It's a good thing that you can add folders to Outlook
Express, because I get way too many e-mails for the
default folders to handle. When I open Outlook Express
for the first time, I always create a Things To Do folder
where I can store e-mail to be worked on later. You can
create folders to help keep your e-mail organized—it's
easy. Right-click Local Folders and click New Folder on
the Shortcut menu. Next, give your new folder a name
and click OK. Now you'll see your new folder listed
under Local Folders.

 MOVE MESSAGES QUICKLY

Now that you've added folders to organize your e-mail, it's time to start using them. To move e-mail, simply drag-and-drop your messages to any folder listed under Local Folders.

 DRAG-AND-DROP TO EDIT

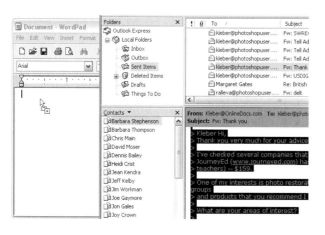

If you want to save an e-mail message as a text file, try this: Open WordPad or Word, then highlight the text of your e-mail in Outlook Express' Preview Pane and drag-and-drop the text into your text editor. Now you can edit and save the message.

CAN'T SPELL?

Let's face it, most of us can't spell. (I can, but then I can do everything—it's a burden.) Well, Outlook Express can help. You can set up Outlook Express to check your spelling automatically before you send messages. To do this, click Tools>Options, then click the Spelling tab. Next, check Always Check Spelling Before Sending, and click OK. You're feeling smarter already, aren't you?

 ## TEACH IT TO SPELL

You can teach Outlook Express to spell. This really comes in handy for frequently used personal and corporate names. Add these names to your Dictionary and Outlook Express won't continually ask you to check their spelling before sending messages. To add words to your Dictionary, click Tools>Options, then click the Spelling tab. Next, click Edit Custom Dictionary and type each word on its own line. Then click File>Save and close the text document.

 ## JUST SHOW ME NEW MESSAGES

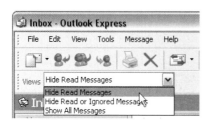

Is your Inbox getting a little crowded? Well if it is, you can hide messages that you've already read to help identify new incoming e-mail. Here's how: Right-click the Toolbar and click Views Bar on the Shortcut menu. Now, select Hide Read Messages in Views and you'll no longer see messages that you've already read.

 ## THAT'S THE FONT FOR ME

It's a good thing that you can customize the text of incoming e-mail, because I have to tell you that some people have a twisted sense of which fonts look good. You can receive e-mail with so many different typefaces and sizes that you're not even sure if they're written in English. Well, you can customize your incoming e-mail so that it displays the same typeface and font size.

To do this, click Tools>Options and click the Read tab in the dialog box. Next, click Fonts, scroll the Proportional Font box to choose your font, then select a Font Size. Click Set as Default, then click OK. Now, all of your incoming messages will have the same look.

NO MAIL FROM YOU

Are you getting annoying e-mail from someone? If you are, you can block the sender's e-mail address, so you won't see their messages. (I do it to all the time just for fun, but that's me; I'm just mean.) Anyway, when you block an e-mail address, any mail received from that address is automatically placed in your Deleted Items folder. You don't ever have to see it.

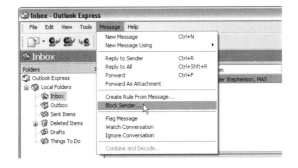

Here's how: Select their e-mail message and click Message>Block Sender. This instantly adds the sender's e-mail address to your Blocked Senders List. To remove someone from the list, click Tools>Message Rules>Blocked Senders List, select the e-mail address, and click Remove. You can also manually add an address to your list using the Blocked Senders List dialog box.

CHECK E-MAIL CONTINUOUSLY

If you check your e-mail throughout the day and have a constant connection to the Internet, then there's no need for you to check manually for new messages. Let Outlook Express automatically check for you. First, click Tools>Options and click the General tab in the dialog box. Now, check Check for New Messages Every __ Minutes and type a number for how often Outlook Express should check for new messages, then click OK. Now, minimize Outlook Express and it will automatically check for new messages.

 GOT MAIL? YOUR NOTIFICATION AREA KNOWS

Now that you've minimized Outlook Express, how do you know if you've received new messages? The Taskbar's Notification area knows. When new messages arrive at your Inbox, the You Have New E-Mail icon will appear informing you that you've received new e-mail.

 QUICK ADD CONTACTS

Here's a quick way to add someone who has sent you e-mail to your Contacts. With their message selected, click Tools>Add Sender to Address Book. That person now appears in your Contacts.

WHO'S ONLINE?

You can quickly make anyone listed in Contacts an Online Contact by right-clicking their name and clicking Set as Online Contact on the Shortcut menu. The contact needs to have a Microsoft .NET Passport to be added as an Online Contact; if they don't, Outlook Express will prompt you to send them an e-mail requesting that they get one. Anyway, once they're set up, you can use Contacts to monitor their online status.

 SAY "HEY" INSTANTLY

If you notice that a Contact is currently online, you can quickly say "Hey." Just right-click the person's name and click Send Instant Message on the Shortcut menu. This will launch Instant Messenger, letting you type and send your message.

 TOO RACY? TURN IT OFF

Okay, you're in the den playing with the kids, having a great time (as usual), and in between giggles, you figure it would be a good time to check your e-mail. Unfortunately, you received e-mail from a spammer who's sent you a message containing adult images—that's great! This is a conversation I could have put off for the next decade.

Well, you can avoid this by turning off the Preview Pane. Click View>Layout, uncheck Show Preview Pane, then click OK. Now, received messages won't display their contents, only that the e-mail was received; however, you can quickly view any e-mail by right-clicking the message and clicking Open on the Shortcut menu.

 DRAG-AND-DROP ATTACHMENTS

If you're attaching files to an e-mail, you can simply drag-and-drop them onto the New Message window. This will instantly attach your files.

CREATE A VCARD

A vCard in Outlook Express is the same as a business card. Once you create a vCard, you can
attach it to your e-mail by clicking Insert>My
Business Card from a New Message window. When
customers receive your e-mail, they can save your
vCard, giving them a digital copy of your contact
info. Here's how to create yours. First create an
entry for yourself in the Address Book, and then
select your name from the Address Book list.
Now, click File>Export and click Business Card
(vCard). Choose a location to save your vCard,
then click Save.

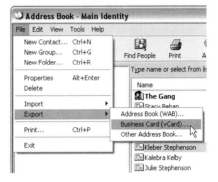

GIVE ME DIRECTIONS

Do you need directions to a contact's
street address? You can get them right
in Outlook Express. Right-click anyone's
name in Contacts and click Properties on
the Shortcut menu. Click the Home or
Business tab and make certain that you've
listed their street address. Now, click View
Map. This will launch your Web browser,
taking you to Microsoft's Expedia Web site
and displaying a map to the address.

 MESSENGER—ARE YOU THERE?

You start a conversation with someone and type and send your message. You wait...nothin'. So, you send an "Are you there?" message. You wait a little longer then send another "Are you there?" message. You're not being ignored; your friend's probably just typing slowly. I have quite a few friends who type slowly—you know who you are. Anyway, wouldn't it be great if you were able to see in real time that they were responding instead of just ignoring you? Now, you can. Just look at the bottom of your Conversation window and you'll see the typing status of your friend. When your friend is responding (typing on the keyboard), you'll see it in real time. So, now you'll know when they're responding and you won't have to send annoying "Are you there?" messages.

 MESSENGER—GIVE ME A BREAK

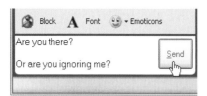

When you press Enter while typing in Messenger, you don't get a line break as you might expect. This actually sends your message. Frustrating, isn't it? Well, next time you need a line break, press Shift-Enter or Ctrl-Enter. This shortcut lets you place line breaks wherever you need 'em.

MESSENGER—DRAG-AND-DROP TO SEND

To quickly send files to someone using Messenger, simply drag-and-drop a file onto the Conversation window. This instantly sends the file to whomever you're chatting with. This action is similar to sending attachments using Outlook Express, only better, because the recipient receives the file instantly and you obtain immediate confirmation of receipt. Messenger will notify you once they've accepted the file.

MESSENGER—.NET ALERTS

.NET Alerts are great! There's just no other way to describe them. You can subscribe to all kinds of alerts: news, sports, travel, finance, and more. To subscribe to new .NET Alerts, first turn on Tabs by clicking Tools>Show Tabs, and select Microsoft .NET Alerts on the Menu Bar. Next, click the .NET tab, click the Go To link, and click Add an Alert. This launches Microsoft's .NET Alerts in your Web browser, where you can subscribe to various content providers. To view Alerts you've subscribed to, click the Provider button.

 MESSENGER—YOU'RE BLOCKED

Eventually, you may find it necessary to block someone from sending you messages. There are many reasons for this, but we're not going to discuss any of them. I'm just going to tell you how to do it.

When you receive a message from someone that you want to block, click Actions>Block on the Menu Bar and that person will no longer be able to send you messages. Unfortunately, there's no way to remove yourself from their Messenger contacts; however, you'll always appear offline to them, making it impossible for them to send you messages. Now, if you decide to forgive this person for whatever they did to you, you can remove them by clicking Tools>Options on the Menu Bar and selecting the Privacy tab in the dialog box. Now, select that person's name in the My Block List and click Allow. This puts them back in the My Allow List.

 MESSENGER—SUPER-FAST GROUPS

Groups are essential for organizing your Messenger contacts, and you can quickly create new groups by right-clicking any existing group and clicking Create New Group on the Shortcut menu. Now, name your new group and you're ready to start adding contacts to it. To view groups, click Tools>Sort Contacts By and select Groups on the Menu Bar.

MESSENGER—QUICKLY ADD CONTACTS TO GROUPS

If there are several contacts that you want to appear in multiple groups, don't just drag-and-drop them. That just moves them. Instead, hold the Ctrl key as you drag-and-drop your contacts. This shortcut creates copies of your contacts rather than moving them.

 MESSENGER—WHAT DID THEY SAY?

This happens all the time. As soon as you've closed the Conversation window, you wish you hadn't because you can't remember your friend's directions, recipe, joke, or whatever. You should have saved your conversation. Oh, you didn't know you could do that? Well, you can. Here's how: Before you close your Conversation window, click File>Save As. Next, name your conversation, then click Save. This saves your entire conversation. Now to view your conversation, simply navigate to the saved file and open it.

 MESSENGER—SEND MESSAGES FROM THE TASKBAR

When signed-in, Windows Messenger always appears in the Notification area of your Taskbar. So, even if Messenger is closed, you can still send an instant message: Just right-click the Messenger icon in the Notification area and, on the Shortcut menu, click Send an Instant Message. This opens a dialog box listing contacts that are currently online. Select the names of the contacts to whom you want to send a message, then click OK. This opens the Conversation window. Now, type your message and click Send to start chatting.

 MESSENGER—MAKE IT A PARTY

A great feature of Windows Messenger is the ability to invite other contacts to your conversations. This really comes in handy when conferencing. To invite other contacts to your current conversation, simply click the Invite Someone to This Conversation link on the sidebar, select additional contacts, and click OK. This will send an invitation for them to join you. You can have up to five people participating in a conversation.

MESSENGER—GET RID OF POP-UPS IN A HURRY

There are annoying pop-ups that, well, pop up from time to time from the Messenger icon in the Notification area. These can be Alerts or advertisements, but they're always annoying, and there's no obvious way to get rid of them. Although eventually they do go away on their own, there is a way to get rid of them on your terms and in a hurry. The next time a pop-up window appears, right-click it. This will instantly close the window.

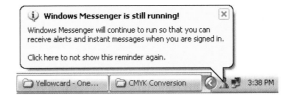

It's a Wrap

WINDOWS MOVIE MAKER 2 TIPS

Windows Movie Maker 2 causes me to get on my soapbox. This is exactly the kind of thing that drives me nuts about

It's a Wrap!

movie making with movie maker 2

Microsoft. They create this killer App that blows away similar programs offered on other platforms, but what good does it do? Nobody even knows that it's on their computer. Other platforms out there sell computers just because of this type of software and theirs isn't as good as Movie Maker. I've actually had friends call and ask me to recommend a movie-making program. Good grief! You've got one of the best I've ever used (at any price) sitting right there in front of you. Microsoft will spend tens of millions of dollars marketing a guy in a butterfly costume—which is fine; I don't have a problem with butterflies—but you'd think they could at least drop a couple of million dollars to advertise one of the best things about XP. It's not like they don't have the cash. Windows XP really does let you do amazing things. Wouldn't it be great if Microsoft would actually tell people about it? Okay, thanks for letting me vent, I feel much better. By the way, if you don't have Movie Maker 2, you can download the free upgrade at microsoft.com.

 ### SUPER-SIZE THE STORYBOARD

Movie Maker's Storyboard view is great. It makes creating movies ridiculously easy; however, the default view is really small—too small. Well, you can actually super-size the Storyboard. Grab the Storyboard's separator bar and drag it up to increase the size of your clips. That's much better!

 ### TRIMMING MADE EASY

Trimming your clips can be a little tricky if you try doing it in the default Timeline view. To be more accurate when trimming your clips, zoom in on the Timeline. Click the Zoom In button or press the Page Down key to see a more detailed view of the Timeline, then click a clip to select it, and pull either end to trim it. You can also watch Movie Maker's monitor (Preview window) as a visual indicator while trimming a clip. The monitor will display exactly where you are on the clip as you trim it. To zoom back out on the Timeline, click the Zoom Out button or the Page Up key.

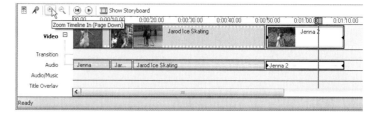

UN-TRIM YOUR CLIPS

Did you get a little carried away trimming your clips? If you did, don't worry, the entire clip is still there. Simply click the clip to select it, drag the trim marker back out, and there's the rest of your clip. Movie Maker doesn't remove the trimmed video from your clips; it only hides it. So, you can always get your original clips back. You can also quickly restore all of your trimmed clips at once by pressing Crtl-Shift-Delete. This shortcut clears all trim marks instantly.

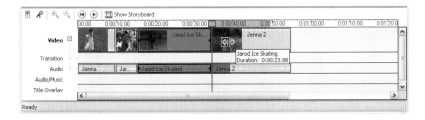

 TRIM A PICTURE

By default, Movie Maker will display an inserted still picture for five seconds. Well, this might not work for your movie. Fortunately, you can trim still pictures exactly the same way as video clips. Click the picture and trim it so that it displays for the appropriate amount of time. You can increase or decrease the display time.

 ## QUICKLY REARRANGE CLIPS

You can rearrange your clips on the Storyboard by simply dragging-and-dropping them in any order you'd like. So, if you decide that the clip on the end of your movie will work better at the beginning, simply drag-and-drop it into place.

 ## CREATE TITLE EFFECTS

 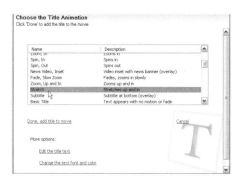

Did you know that you could add effects to your titles? You can. Pretty cool, huh? Create a title for your movie by clicking Tasks on the Toolbar then, on the Movie Tasks Pane under Edit Movie, click Make titles or credits.

Next, select the type of title or credit you want to create, and then type your text, but when you're finished, don't click Done. Instead, click the Choose the Title Animations link under More options. Now, select an animation for your title—you have a ton to choose from. After you've selected an animation, click the Done, Add Title to Movie link and your animated title is inserted into your movie.

QUICK CHANGE TITLE TEXT

If you realize you misspelled one or even
several words in your title, you don't have
to trash it and start all over again. Simply
double-click the title in the Storyboard or
Timeline view and the Title Pane opens with
the title's text displayed and ready to be
edited. When you're finished making your
corrections, click Done.

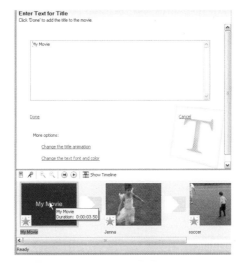

SNAG A STILL SHOT

If you want to capture a still shot from a video
clip, you can. Here's how: Use the Timeline
or the monitor's (Preview window) Seek Bar
to locate the image that you want to capture
from your clip, then click the Take Picture icon
(see image). Movie Maker will ask you where
you'd like to save the picture on your hard
drive. Choose a location and click Save in the
dialog box. Movie Maker will save the capture
as a JPEG and automatically import it into
the source clip's Collection. The picture will
appear in the Collection's Contents Pane. Now,
simply drag-and-drop the picture anywhere on
the Storyboard.

 FREEZE FRAME

The previous tip is great for snagging still images, but here's a way to put the tip to good use: Create a freeze frame effect for your movie. Split the clip at the same point on the Timeline where you captured the still image by clicking Split Clip on the monitor (Preview window). This splits the clip into two clips on the Timeline. Next, insert the picture that you captured earlier in between the two clips. Now, preview your video. Isn't that a great effect?

 AUDIO ONLY

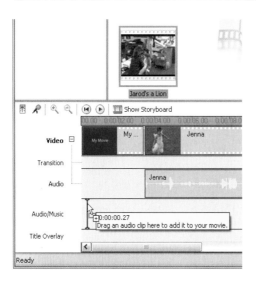

Movie Maker makes it a breeze to use only the audio portion of a video clip. Drag-and-drop the video clip onto the Audio/Music Track of the Timeline. Now, you can see the clip's audio on the Timeline, but there's no video. Very quick and very cool!

GET RID OF THE AUDIO

Well, if you can get rid of the video portion of a clip, it's only fair that you should be able to get rid of a clip's audio and just keep the video, right? Right! Here's how: On the Timeline, right-click the audio portion of your video clip on the Audio Track of the Timeline and click Mute on the Shortcut menu. Now, when you preview your movie, the video clip's sound is removed.

AUTOMOVIE

Movie Maker is such a great App that you don't have to know how to create a movie. If you're in a hurry, or just don't feel like using the Timeline, then let Movie Maker do it for you. Import your clips into a new or existing Collection. Next, open the Collection so that you can view the Collection's clips in the Contents Pane. Then, click Tools>AutoMovie on the Menu Bar. This opens the AutoMovie Pane, which allows you to select from several different styles for your movie. Select a style, then click Done, Edit Movie. Movie Maker actually creates your movie for you, complete with splits, transitions, titles, and credits. When AutoMovie's finished, the layout of your new movie appears on the Timeline. This allows you to edit any part of the movie quickly, then save it.

ADD BACKGROUND MUSIC

You can add background music to your movie by dragging a music file from the Contents Pane anywhere onto the Audio/Music Track on the Timeline. Then, simply drag the file into position and trim it to match a video clip or your entire movie. Keep in mind that when you add background music to your movie, it plays at a 50/50 volume level with the existing clip or movie's Audio Track. You can, however, adjust the background's audio to play louder or softer than 50/50 by right-clicking the Audio Track on the Timeline and clicking Volume on the Shortcut menu. Now, slide the Volume control in the dialog box to adjust the background's music to play louder or softer, and then click OK.

To add a nice touch to your background music, right-click the background Audio Track and click Fade Out on the Shortcut menu. This will automatically fade out instead of abruptly ending the music at the end of the audio file's Timeline. This technique can also be used to control the volume of any sound effect or narration.

NARRATE YOUR MOVIES

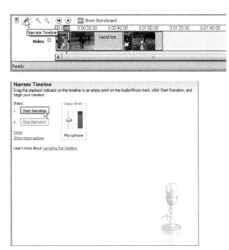

Do you need to explain to your audience what they're seeing? You can by adding narrations to your movie. Here's how: Drag the Timeline slider to the location on your movie where you want to begin the narration. Next, click Narrate Timeline. Then, on the Narrate Timeline Pane, click Start Narration and speak into your computer's microphone. Click Stop Narration when finished. Your narration now appears on the Audio/Music Track on the Timeline.

GETTIN' GEEKY WITH TRANSITIONS

Okay, we all know that you create transitions by simply dragging-and-dropping them into the transition window between clips on the Storyboard. And, you've probably always stopped there, not realizing that you can add some pretty cool effects to transitions. Try this: Highlight a transition on the Storyboard, click Tasks on the Toolbar, then click Make Titles or Credits on the Movie Tasks Pane. Next, click Add Title on the Selected Clip in the Timeline, then type your text, and add a title animation. When you're finished, click Done, Add Title to Movie, and you've just applied text and text animations to a transition.

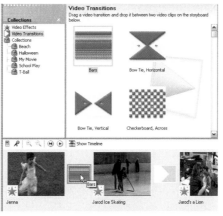

CROSS-FADE CLIPS

This is my favorite hidden-effects trick in Movie Maker. You can cross-fade any two clips to add a truly professional transition between them, and it's really easy. Here's how to do it: Grab a clip on

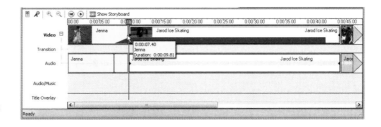

the Timeline and drag it onto the clip directly to the left. You'll see a blue transition bar that indicates the length of the cross-fade. When you have the clip where you want it, drop it. Now, preview your movie. Check out that transition. Very nice!

 DOUBLE TIME

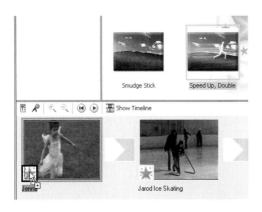

Smudge Stick   Speed Up, Double

Show Timeline

Jenna   Jarod Ice Skating

Here's a nice way to speed things up. You can double the playback speed of any clip on the Storyboard by applying the Speed Up, Double effect to a clip. To add the effect, click Tasks on the Toolbar and click View Video Effects on the Movie Tasks Pane. Then, drag-and-drop the Speed Up, Double effect onto a clip on the Story-board. Now preview your movie. That's fast, isn't it?

Want to make it play even faster? Apply the effect again. You reapply effects to clips (up to six times) by repeatedly dragging-and-dropping them onto a clip. This technique is actually useful and works especially well when lightening a clip by using the Brightness, Increase effect. Keep applying the effect to increase the brightness of a dark clip.

 GETTING PRECISE WITH THE TIMELINE

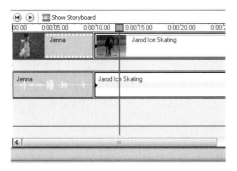

Show Storyboard
00.00   0:00:05.00   0:00:10.00   0:00:15.00   0:00:20.00   0:00:
Jenna   Jarod Ice Skating
Jenna   Jarod Ice Skating

Press-and-hold the Alt key and then press the left or right arrow key to move the Timeline forward or backward exactly one frame at a time. This allows you to trim your clips to precise locations on the Timeline and helps to identify the best frame of a video clip for still-shot captures.

BACK TO THE BEGINNING

You'll find when creating movies that you're constantly stopping and then restarting previews, and it can only help to do this quickly. So, to jump back to the beginning of your movies, press Ctrl-Q or the Home key. Both of these shortcuts will quickly return the Timeline to the beginning of your movie.

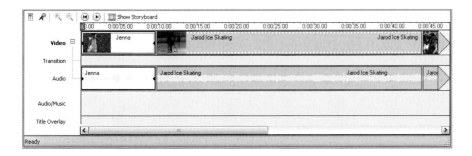

QUICK FADES

Fade In and Fade Out are a couple of my favorite effects and apparently they're also favorites of the Movie-Maker programmers, because they gave us a quick shortcut to them. To add a fade-in or fade-out effect to your clips quickly, simply right-click any clip on the Storyboard or Timeline and click Fade In, Fade Out, or both on the Shortcut menu. Preview your movie to see the effect.

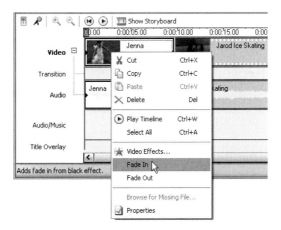

 ## DON'T SPLIT MY CLIP

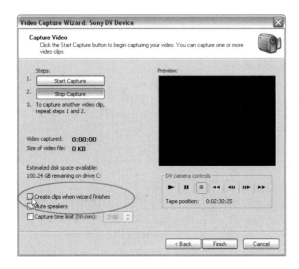

By default, Movie Maker automatically separates your video into multiple clips as they're imported into a Collection. You can avoid this by clearing the Create Clips When Wizard Finishes checkbox on the Video Capture Wizard. Now, your video will be imported as a single video clip.

 ## DO-IT-YOURSELF CLIPS

Okay, you used the previous tip to import your video into Movie Maker as a single clip; but now you've realized that there are several places throughout the movie where you'd like to create transitions and apply special effects. What are you going to do? Don't worry, try this: Simply drag the Timeline to the location on your movie where you'd like to insert a transition or special effect and click Split Clip on the monitor (Preview window). This splits the movie into two clips on the Timeline. Repeat this as many times as necessary to create as many clips as you want.

SHARE YOUR CLIPS

Movie Maker lets you share clips between your Collections. For example, let's say you have five Collections of imported video clips and you want to use a few clips from each Collection to make a movie. Well, you can and here's how: Click Collections on the Toolbar, then right-click the Collections folder on the Collections Pane and click New Collection on the Shortcut menu. Next, name your new folder and just start dragging-and-dropping clips from other Collections into your new Collections folder. Now your clips are sorted and ready to be made into a movie. *Note*: You can drag-and-drop copies of a clip by holding the Ctrl key when moving them into the new folder. This keyboard tip copies the clip to the new folder instead of just moving it.

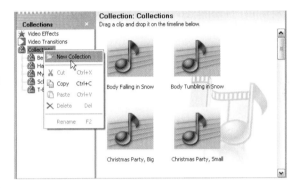

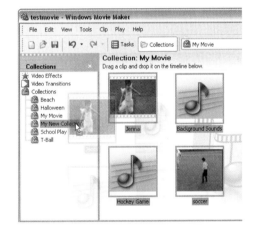

Hacked Off

Those Annoying Things You Do

There's not a lot about XP that really annoys me, but the things that do, really do. It's amazing what sets me

Hacked Off

those annoying things you do

off. I can just be doing my thing in XP and open a search and BAM! There's that dog, just sittin' there waggin' his tail. What does this puppy have to do with searching my computer? Once again, those engineers over at Microsoft are "cute-ing" me to death. If you want to impress me, stick a Tomahawk Cruise missile on there. Now, that's my kind of search. Come on guys, show a little attitude for cryin' out loud.

In this chapter, I've also thrown in a few tips on how to really tweak your friends. I have to admit I started to get a little carried away here and had to scale it back. I realized that I could do some really mean things to someone's computer and had nightmares for a week. I mean really, how could anyone do those kinds of things, and to a computer? It was awful. I'm not proud of myself.

 YES, I REALLY WANT TO DELETE

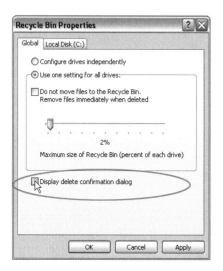

Oh, I appreciate the fact that Windows thinks I may have been kidding when I tried deleting that file, but it's just gotta stop asking me. Once and for all—Yes, Yes, Yes, I really want to delete that! Here's how to show Windows that you're serious too. Right-click the Recycle Bin's icon and click Properties on the Shortcut menu. Next, click the Global tab in the dialog box, uncheck Display Delete Confirmation Dialog, and then click Apply.

 I KNOW, I INSTALLED IT

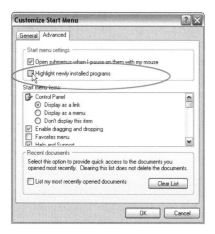

Have you noticed that XP highlights newly installed programs on the All Programs menu? Isn't that nervy? This one really gets me; I know I've installed a program. I did it, and I even know where it's located. Yep, believe it or not, I've used Windows before. I really wish Microsoft would stop assuming that we've never used Windows before. Honestly, how many people out there are brand-new to Windows, maybe 20 or so? Well, let's turn this off and maybe I won't feel like my OS thinks I'm an idiot.

Right-click Start and click Properties on the Shortcut menu. Click the Start Menu tab in the dialog box and click Customize. Next, click the Advanced tab, uncheck Highlight Newly Installed Programs, then click OK.

STOP PRINTING

Don't ever try to get to your
Printer's folder to stop a print job.
You'll never make it in time. It's
buried somewhere in the Control
Panel. By the time you get there,
your printer will have already
finished printing, sorting, stapling,

and stacking your documents. Fortunately, there's a much faster way.

When you send files to your printer you'll notice a Printer icon appears in the Taskbar's
Notification Area. Double-click this icon, which will open your Printer folder. Now right-
click the print job that you want to stop and click Cancel on the Shortcut menu.

 DON'T REPORT ME

By default, XP will request that you send an error
report to Microsoft whenever you experience a
problem. Yikes, why in the world would anyone
want to do this? I don't know how to explain exactly
why I think this is a bad idea and be kind, so I
won't. Let me just say that I really don't know how
an error with my computer's OS and software is
going to help Microsoft produce a better product.
So, I'm going to politely decline and turn this feature off so that I don't have a mini-meltdown every
time I see it.

If you'd like to avoid mini-meltdowns too, do the
following: Click Start then the Control Panel. Next,
click Performance and Maintenance>System, then
click the Advanced tab in the dialog box, and click
Error Reporting. Now, select Disable Error Reporting
and click OK.

 A LESS-FRIENDLY SEARCH

As discussed in this chapter's introduction, the Search puppy has to go. Here's how: Click Start then Search. Next, click the Change Preferences link under What Do You Want to Search For? and then click Without an Animated Search Character. See ya, pooch.

 I'LL UPDATE MYSELF

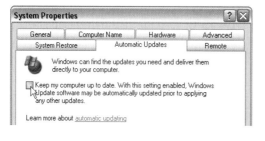

I kind of resent being interrupted by my computer, especially to inform me about updates. I mean, if my computer's going to interrupt me, make it good and tell me it's time for lunch, not that there may be some nondescript update available for my OS. I'd rather have my computer scanned for needed updates when I choose. There's just something freaky about my OS doing this in the background. I prefer to check for updates manually. If you do too, click Start then Control Panel. Next, click Performance and Maintenance>System. Now, click the Automatic Updates tab in the dialog box, uncheck Keep My Computer Up to Date..., then click OK.

NO MORE POP-UPS

XP is a power-user's OS, but I really don't think
the developers at Microsoft get this. All the little
"helpful" extras, such as pop-up descriptions in XP,
just seem unnecessary. They're more in the way
and a distraction than helpful, but at least you can
turn 'em off. Click Start then Control Panel. Next,
click Appearance and Themes, and then Folder
Options. Click the View tab in the dialog box,
scroll the Advanced settings and uncheck Show
Pop-Up Description for Folder and Desktop Items,
then click OK.

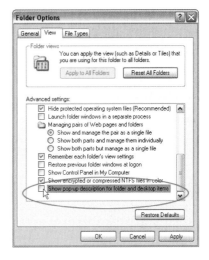

 ## BIGGER, SMALLER—THEY'RE THE SAME

Double-click the volume icon in the Taskbar's
Notification Area. You see your Volume Control,
right? Now, press Ctrl-S and you see a much
smaller Volume Control, right? What's up with
that? It's exactly the same volume control only
smaller. Why is this even an option?

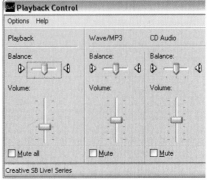

 I'M DISTRACTED

Windows Messenger is a killer App! I use it constantly. There's only one problem though. Everyone I know also uses it constantly, and if I'm online, everyone knows it. Now, I'm easily distracted—I don't know why, but it's a problem. So, if people start sending me instant messages, before you know it, I'm chatting away completely forgetting about whatever I was working on.

Well, you can change your online status to help prevent this type of distraction by right-clicking the Windows Messenger icon in the Taskbar's Notification Area. Next, point to My Status and click Busy on the Shortcut menu. Now, Messenger is still available to you, but you won't be distracted by incoming messages.

 WHY WOULD I WANT TO RESTART?

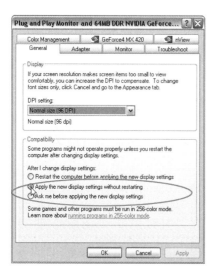

Have you ever changed your Display settings and been asked to restart your computer before applying the new settings? Yeah, me too. Of course I don't want to restart my computer. I'd rather lick the sidewalk than restart my computer. Do you know how long that takes? Way too long. That's how long. As a matter of fact, Windows should never do anything to my computer that forces me to restart. I cringe every time I even consider turning off my computer. In fact, I usually don't turn it off, just to avoid having to turn it back on. If you get this should-be-error message when you change your Display settings, do this: Right-click the Desktop and click Properties on the Shortcut menu. Next, click the Settings tab in the dialog box and click Advanced. Click the General tab, select Apply the New Display Settings Without Restarting, then click OK.

BEAT YOUR CD PLAYER TO THE PUNCH

Here's a new annoying feature, courtesy of XP. When you insert a CD, you get an AutoPlay dialog box that pops up asking what you'd like to do with the CD and listing several options, depending on the CD's contents. Well, thanks for holding my hand through this whole inserting-the-CD thing, but I think I'd rather go it alone. But that's just me. I'm a rebel. If you're a rebel too and prefer to go it alone, then you can beat XP to the punch and tell it what to do with your CDs before you insert them. Click Start then My Computer. Right-click your CD drive's icon and click Properties on the Shortcut menu. Now, click the AutoPlay tab in the dialog box and click Select an action to perform. Use the drop-down menu to select different CD types and then assign an action to them. Now, when you insert a CD you won't see the AutoPlay pop-up.

 WHY CAN'T I DRAG-AND-DROP IT? YOU CAN, BUT IT'S WEIRD

A friend called me with a problem he was having and I have to admit, it baffled me for a couple of minutes. He opened the Desktop Toolbar on the Taskbar and tried to drag-and-drop files to it, but couldn't. I thought,

"Rookie," until I tried it and it didn't work for me either. But, how could this be? Sure it's a Toolbar, but it's still a folder (Desktop or not). I shouldn't have any trouble dragging files to it. Well, I discovered that you can, it's just a little weird. Start by opening the Desktop Toolbar—right-click the Taskbar, point to Toolbars, and click Desktop. Now, open a folder and try dragging any file onto the Toolbar. You can't, but here's the trick: Move the file to the right of the word "Desktop," now you can drop it. Why can't you just drop it on the folder's name? I have no idea. Annoying isn't it?

 ## SCIENTIFIC CALCULATOR?

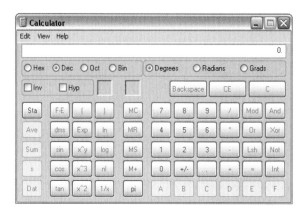

Have you ever used a Scientific Calculator? Do you know anyone who has ever used a Scientific Calculator? What the heck is a Scientific Calculator? Did you even know that you have a Scientific Calculator? Yes, you do. You can see it by opening the Calculator and clicking View>Scientific. Now, hurry, close it. If you look at it long enough it'll make you feel stupid. That's just annoying.

 ## ANNOY OTHERS—FREAKY DESKTOP

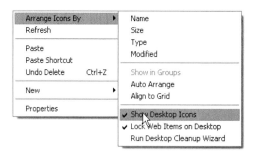

This is mild but very freaky. Right-click the Desktop, point to Arrange Icons By, and click (uncheck) Show Desktop Icons. Now, they're gone! Freaky, isn't it? This should keep 'em guessing for a while. If they figure it out, you can keep the fun going; just reapply it every time they leave the room.

ANNOY OTHERS—MY DOCUMENTS ARE GONE!

Have you ever seen your friend or co-worker completely dazed and confused? If not, it's probably
about time that you did. This look can easily be
achieved by hiding My Documents. Click Start, then
right-click My Documents, and click Properties on the
Shortcut menu. Next, click the General tab in the
dialog box, check Hidden, then click OK. When the
confirmation dialog pops up, select Apply changes to
this folder, subfolders, and files, and click OK.

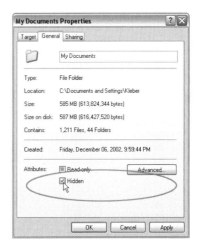

Now, here's what gets 'em every time. Even
though you told Windows to hide the My Documents
folder, it won't. (I don't know why.) So, because he
can see the folder, your friend will never think that it
could simply be that the folder "somehow" became
hidden. But every folder and file in My Documents is
hidden. In other words, gone! Yep, he's starting to
get that dazed and confused look. Can you see it?

 ANNOY OTHERS—NOTHING BUT SHORTCUT MENUS

Want to get a co-worker on the bad side of
your IT person? Switch her mouse buttons.
Now every time, she clicks the left-mouse
button, all she'll get is a Shortcut menu.
She'll think that her mouse has gone bad,
for sure. After the IT person tries two or
three mice without fixing the problem and
figures out what's really happening, it'll be
too late for your friend. The tech won't

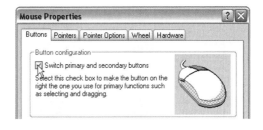

think it's funny. Yep, it'll be a cold day in you-know-where before she gets assistance
again. In fact, she might just be working on a 386 (very old and crappy) machine by the
end of the week.

To switch the mouse buttons, click Start then Control Panel. Next, click Printers and
Other Hardware>Mouse. Now, depending on the mouse driver, click the Buttons tab in the
dialog box, click Switch the Primary and Secondary Buttons, and then click OK.

 ANNOY OTHERS—CAN YOU SEE ME NOW?

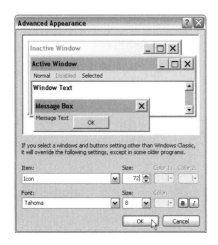

You know, I think the icons on my friend's Desktop are just too small. Yeah, way too small, let's amp 'em up and see what happens. Will he buy a new video card, a new monitor, re-install Windows, or see an eye doctor? Let's try it and find out. Right-click the Desktop and click Properties on the Shortcut menu. Next, click the Appearance tab in the dialog box and click Advanced. Select Icon on the Item menu, crank-up the size (up to 72 pixels), then click OK. Wow, those are pretty big icons. I'm guessing a re-install is in order.

 ANNOY OTHERS—SHUT DOWN AT STARTUP

Here's an annoying tip that could actually give someone an ulcer. In Chapter 5, I showed you how to create a shutdown shortcut for your Desktop ("Shortcut to Shut Down"). Well, let's have some fun with a co-worker. *Important: Make absolutely certain that you can start their computer in Safe Mode before attempting this, or it won't be funny at all.*

Copy the Shutdown Shortcut and paste it into his Start-up folder, usually located at C:\Documents and Settings\ User Name\Start Menu\Programs\Startup. Now, every time he starts up his computer, it will immediately shut down as soon as Windows tries to launch. He'll never be able to launch Windows. Pretty funny, huh? Actually, this isn't really that funny. At least not to your victim, so please make sure that you're close by when he starts pounding on his computer and cussing the Internet for giving him a virus.

To undo this, you'll have to launch Windows in Safe Mode (usually by pressing F8 as the computer starts up). After Windows has launched in Safe Mode, delete the file from Startup and restart the computer.

ANNOY OTHERS—LAUNCH EVERYTHING AT ONCE

This isn't damaging but it is annoying. She'll be pushing keys left and right trying to stop this deluge of Apps. It cracks me up every time. Similar to the previous tip, copy shortcuts of as many Apps as possible and put them in your friend's Startup folder. The more you put in there, the funnier it is—trust me on this. You just can't launch too many Apps at the same time—on your friend's computer that is. It's not funny at all on your computer.

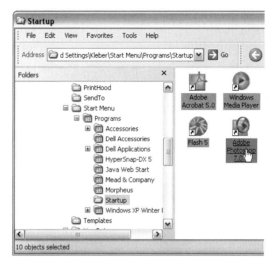

Doh!

TROUBLESHOOTING

TIPS

Okay, I'm sure Windows has never crashed on you or caused you any problems; but when (I mean if) you ever do have a

Doh!

troubleshooting . . . smash forehead on keyboard to continue

problem, it's your fault. Please step away from the computer. You clearly have no idea what you're doing. Just kidding! You can sit back down. There's just nothing good about troubleshooting. We don't want to do it and feel that we shouldn't have to anyway. My computer's supposed to work perfectly—all the time! It's not as if I did anything to cause this. (Keyboards are supposed to be waterproof, right?) Well, I have only two pieces of advice when it comes to troubleshooting. First, be patient; whatever the problem, you can fix it. Secondly, don't actually smash your forehead on the keyboard. It doesn't work. I've tried it. I just got a nasty bump and it didn't fix a thing.

 THREE-FINGER SALUTE

Folks, if you remember only one keyboard shortcut in XP, this is the one, because eventually you're gonna need it. This tip is truly for those of you who are new to Windows. Everyone else who's been using Windows for at least six months has already learned the Windows Ctrl-Alt-Delete three-finger salute. This is not what I'd consider a killer tip; however I just wouldn't feel that I was doing my job if I didn't include it. It's been too much a part of my life to leave out. So, here we go.

Believe it or not, eventually a program might freeze on you or Windows will just inexplicably stop responding. When this happens, press Ctrl-Alt-Delete on your keyboard. This opens the Windows Task Manager. Now, click the Applications tab in the dialog box and select the program that's not responding, then click End Task. If this still doesn't do the trick, you can shut down by clicking Shut Down>Restart on the Task Manager's Menu Bar.

 WHERE'S MY SCANDISK?

I was probably using Windows XP for about two weeks before I went looking for the comfort of my trusted ScanDisk. I thought I was going to be sick—I couldn't find it. ScanDisk wasn't there. Well, I'm here to save you from going through this trauma. ScanDisk isn't included in Windows XP; instead you get the improved Check Disk tool. You can use the Error-Checking tool to check for system file errors and bad sectors on your hard drives. To use Check Disk, click Start>My Computer, then right-click the hard drive you want to check, and click Properties on the Shortcut menu. Next, click the Tools tab in the dialog box and click Check Now (under Error Checking).

KNOWLEDGE CAN MAKE YOU SMARTER

Without a doubt, the best feature in the Help and Support Center is its online access to Microsoft's Knowledge Base. The Knowledge Base is Help on steroids—its über-Help. Just about any kind of problem you're having with Windows has probably been addressed here. Which is great, but what's really useful is its hidden power. You can use the Knowledge Base to find help for practically any software title that Microsoft develops. Here's how: Click Start>Help and Support and click the Set Search Options link directly under the Search text box. Next, click to expand the menu for Microsoft Knowledge Base and select the program that you need help with. Now, uncheck Suggested Topics and Full-Text Search Matches to search only the Knowledge Base, then type a search term, and click the Start Searching arrow button. There ya go, instant help for all of your favorite software. Just keep in mind that you must be online to search Microsoft's Knowledge Base.

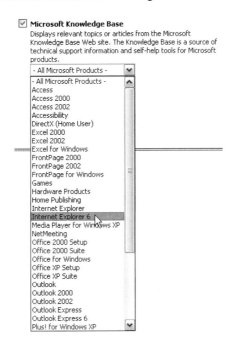

 AM I CONNECTED?

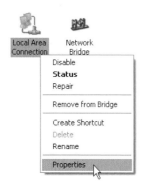

There's a really quick way to tell whether your connection to the Internet or network is active: View its status in the Taskbar's Notification area. Click Start>My Network Places and click View Network Connections under Network Tasks. Next, right-click the Local Area Connection or any network icon and click Properties on the Shortcut menu. Check Show Icon in Notification Area When Connected, and then click OK. Now, you can view your network connections on the Taskbar. You'll never be left hanging again. If your Web page isn't loading or if you're not able to access files on the server, you'll know whether it's your computer melting down, or it's simply a bad connection. And you'll know it instantly, as both monitors on the Connections icon light up when the connection is active. You won't have to stare at a blank Web page or watch your hourglass spin for five minutes before figuring out that you may not be connected.

 GIVE IT A BOOST

Remember when Mom would remind you to clean your room? You hated it, didn't you? Well, I'm here to bring back the good ol' days because I'm definitely gonna get after you to clean your computer. Over time, your computer can get cluttered with all kinds of junk, much like toys under the bed and dirty clothes in the closet—you can't necessarily see the mess, but it's there. Disk Cleanup can free up a ton of space by searching your hard drive for files, such as unnecessary program files, temporary files, and cached Internet files, and deleting them. To run Disk Cleanup, click Start>All Programs>Accessories>System Tools>Disk Cleanup For, then select the drive you want to clean, and click OK. The search will return a list of files that can be deleted safely. Click OK to delete the files.

FEELING SLUGGISH?

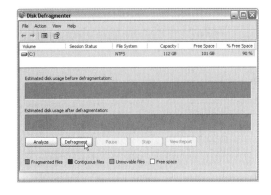

If Windows begins to get sluggish, you probably need to defrag your hard drive. As you install and remove programs, add files and delete files, your hard drive can become a little fragmented—this means that parts of your files and Apps become a little scattered on your drive. This makes your hard drive take longer to locate files and respond more slowly. You can get Windows back up to speed by running Disk Defragmenter and getting your files back together. Here's how: Click Start>All Programs>Accessories>SystemTools>Disk Defragmenter. Now, select the drive you want to defrag and click Defragment. Oh, by the way, it's a good idea to plan your vacation around this—it might actually be finished when you get back. In other words, it takes a long time.

 ## WE'RE COMPATIBLE

You love XP, but you're simply devastated that you can no longer run your favorite game—*Invasion of the Mutant Space Bats of Doom*, an actual game made for Windows 95. Well, bring back the Bats! They can invade once again. You've just got to make your old game compatible. You can get older games and programs to run on XP by using the Program Compatibility Wizard. The Wizard lets you test your older programs in different Windows environments; in other words, if you have a program designed to run in Windows 95, then you can set its compatibility mode to Windows 95 so that it runs in XP.

To set a program's compatibility, click Start>All Programs>Accessories>Program Compatibility Wizard. When the Wizard opens, simply follow the instructions to select your program and set its compatibility.

 IT COULD BE HUNG UP

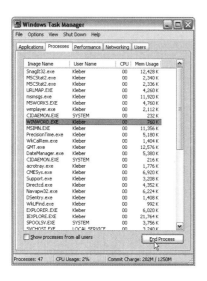

Have you ever tried to launch a program and nothing happened. Tried it again—nothin'! Again—nothin'! Well, don't start reinstalling the program just yet. It might simply be hung up. The next time this happens, press Ctrl-Alt-Delete to open Task Manager. Click the Processes tab in the dialog box, select the App that you were trying to launch, and click End Process. Now, try to launch the program again.

 SAVE SEARCHES

You go through a lot of trouble to search for something on your computer. You may have to perform several different searches using various keywords to find what you're looking for. Of course, just as soon as you close the search window, you wish you hadn't, because you can't remember where the file was, and you can't remember how you found it to begin with. Well, that bites! Fortunately, this will never happen to you again, because you're going to save your search results. Here's how: Click Start>Search and perform a search (for whatever). Once you've found the desired results, click File>Save Search on the Menu Bar. Now, pick a location on your hard drive to save your search results and click Save.

HELP AND SUPPORT FAVORITES

You already know how
frustrating and time-
consuming locating files
using Search can be, but
have you ever searched
for info using XP's Help
and Support Center? Oh
yeah, this is user friendly!
You could be digging for

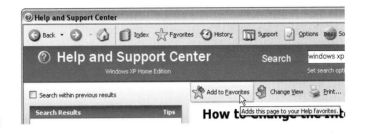

hours before you find what you're looking for. Apparently the developers at Microsoft knew
this, because they were kind enough to give Help and Support its own Favorite—I bet you
never noticed it. Try this: Once you've finally finished a search, don't close the window;
you'll never find it again. Instead, click Add to Favorites, which will save your search
results to Help and Support's Favorites. Now, to get back to your search results, simply
open the Help and Support Center, click Favorites on the Toolbar, and there it is.

I CAN'T MOVE MY TOOLBARS

Can't move your Toolbars? There's a simple
explanation for this: You're using a pirated copy
of XP and Microsoft's been notified. Yep, you're a
criminal—just kidding. (I bet that made a couple
of you sweat.) Actually, your Toolbars are locked,
so right-click the Windows Taskbar or the Toolbar
that's giving you trouble and uncheck Lock the
Toolbars on the Shortcut menu. Now, you should
be able to move them wherever you'd like. If you
still can't move 'em, then you really are using a
pirated copy of XP and you're a bad person.

 I WISH I COULD GO BACK

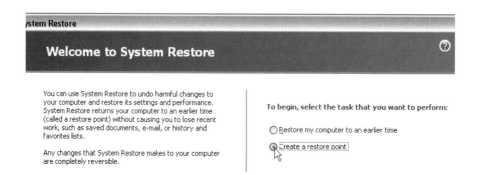

This is a simple task that can save you tons of frustration and make you look like a genius. Before installing or removing programs, or making significant changes to your Operating System (OS), you should consider creating a Restore Point. A Restore Point saves the state of your computer at the time you create it. So, when you download and install that must-have beta game from the Internet on your office server and it brings down the entire network, you can quickly restore the computer to the way it was before you installed the game. You can go back. Your boss will think you're a complete idiot for installing it in the first place, but she'll think you're a genius for covering your you-know-what by creating a Restore Point first.

Here's how to do it: Click Start>Help and Support and click System Restore (under Additional Resources), which launches the System Restore Wizard. Now, select Create a Restore Point, click Next, then give your Restore Point a name, and click Create. Now, if the changes you made to your computer cause problems, simply come back to the same Wizard and select Restore My Computer to an Earlier Time, and select your Restore Point to get back to normal.

PROTECT FILES FROM SYSTEM RESTORE

When is using System Restore to
restore your computer a bad thing?
When it removes files and folders
that you wanted to keep. Any new
files or folders that were added to
your computer after the Restore
date you select are subject to
removal. This is not the point of
System Restore. You can protect
files from System Restore, however,
by moving any files that you feel

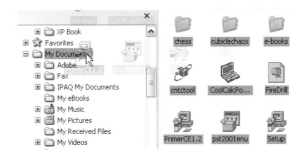

may be affected by a System Restore to your My Documents folder. System Restore doesn't
affect the My Documents folder; that is, whatever's in My Documents before a system
restore will still be there afterward.

DON'T JUST CLICK OK

I bet you've received an error message in Windows and tried to remember what it read (which never works),
or quickly looked for a pen to write
down the error. We all have. I also
bet that the entire time you were
writing, you were thinking, "There's
got to be a better way to do this."
Well you were right. There is a better

way to do this; you just didn't know about it until now.

   The next time an error dialog box pops up, press Ctrl-C. This keyboard shortcut copies
the text of the error message. Open Notepad, WordPad, or any text editor, and paste the
error's message (Ctrl-V). Now you can save the message for reference. This really comes
in handy when contacting technical support or when using Microsoft's Knowledge Base
for help, because you can use keywords, specific error numbers, or codes from the error
message to help identify the problem.

SAVE THE BLUE SCREEN OF DEATH

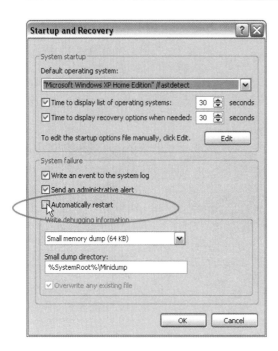

When things really go bad in Windows, you're going to get the worst of all errors: the Stop error—also known as the Blue Screen of Death. This is usually caused by a bad device driver and can be frightening the first time you see it. But don't be afraid; it tells you exactly what the problem is. Depending on your setup, the Stop error will quickly disappear and your computer will automatically restart. Well, that's just great! Not only is the error in geek-speak, but it also disappeared as you were writing it down.

Let's stop the insanity and make the Blue Screen of Death work for us. First, turn off Automatic Restart under System Failure by clicking Start>Control Panel>Performance and Maintenance>System, then clicking the Advanced tab in the dialog box. Next, click Settings under Startup and Recovery, uncheck Automatically Restart, then click OK. Now, the Stop error will appear indefinitely. The next time you receive a Stop error, make special note of the error's name, code, and driver details. Use this information when contacting technical support or when searching Microsoft's Knowledge Base.

HOW MUCH SPACE DO I NEED?

Here's a simple tip that will save you a lot of time and aggravation. A standard CD will hold 650 MB of data, so before you begin copying files to your CD/RW drive, calculate how much disk space you're going to need. If your files are all contained in a single folder, right-click the folder, click Properties on the Shortcut menu, then click the General tab in the dialog box, and look at the folder's size. This will tell you exactly how large the combined files in the folder are. If your files exceed 650 MB, you'll know it beforehand and can make adjustments before you start copying to your CD.

TRASH THE GARBAGE

You know, I've never really understood the purpose of the Windows Temp folder. I mean, I get why it's there and what it does; I just don't understand why it holds onto files like grim death. Basically, just about any time you install new software, Windows shuts down improperly, or a program or Windows crashes, files will be created in the Windows Temp folder. These files are useless. You can safely delete them without damaging Windows. There's my point: Why in the world doesn't Windows do a better job of eliminating this garbage? If Windows ever begins giving you trouble, check your Windows Temp folders. I've actually seen thousands of files in Temp folders consuming Gigs of drive space. That's just crazy!

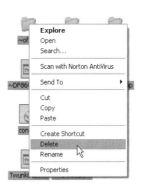

Your Temp folders are in two locations, C:\Windows\Temp and C:\Documents and Settings\Username\Local Settings\Temp. Local Settings, under Documents and Settings, is hidden by default, so you'll have to enable Show Hidden Files and Folders in Folder Options to see this folder. Anyway, navigate to these Temp folders and delete the files inside them. If you've never visited your Temp folders before, you'll probably be shocked at what you find.

 PREFETCH?

Windows is at it again. The Temp folders just weren't eating up enough of your hard drive space, so Microsoft's developers thought it would be a good idea to create more folders that do basically the same thing. Hey, thanks! No, really, thanks. We can't possibly have enough disk-eating folders. And to make it worse, they're giving them new names. Yeah, they know that we're onto the whole Temp folder thing, so this new one's called Prefetch.

Prefetch functions differently from the Windows Temp folder; however, like the Temp folders, it will hang on to your Trash forever—if you let it. Prefetch tends to get pretty cluttered with Application files no longer being used, so you should occasionally empty this folder. (You should find Prefetch at C:Windows\Prefetch.) And, don't worry; you can't damage Windows by removing these files. Any deleted files that Windows needs will be re-created automatically.

 10% IS TOO MUCH

Do you need more disk space? I do too. We all do. Well, believe it or not, your Recycle Bin does more than eat your Trash; it steals your disk space too. By default, Windows reserves a whopping 10% of your hard drive for your Recycle Bin. Yeah, 10%! My hard drive is a little larger than 100 GB. Now, I'm not Stephen Hawking, but I can quickly calculate—even without breaking out the scientific calculator—that my Recycle Bin has reserved more than 10 GB of my hard drive to hold my Trash. My first network of computers didn't have that much disk space. And if you don't routinely empty your Recycle Bin, you could very quickly be using Gigs of disk space without even realizing it.

I just want a Trash can, not an entire landfill. So, let's see if we can't reclaim a little (or a lot) of this disk space. Right-click the Recycle Bin and click Properties on the Shortcut menu. Next, click the Global tab in the dialog box and move the slider to a more reasonable percentage, say 1% or 2%, then click OK.

STAY UP TO DATE WITH UPDATE

Windows Update is the single best tool for main-
taining your computer's performance. Windows
Update will automatically scan your system and
inform you of OS, driver, and critical updates
available for your computer. Once Windows
Update scans your system, it returns a list of
recommended updates that you can select to
install. This really is a great feature that will
leave you wishing everything in Windows worked
this well. You can check for updates by clicking
Start>Control Panel>Windows Update—located
under See Also on the Tasks Panel. Once Windows
Update launches, click the Scan for Updates link to
begin. You must be online to use Windows Update.

 ## I FORGOT MY PASSWORD, NOW WHAT?

Okay, this is always pure torture. You've
forgotten your password, and now you can't
get into Windows—nice. Well, you can
either reinstall Windows or insert your
password disk to create a new password and
get back into Windows. Oh, you didn't create a password-reset disk, did you? That's
really too bad because if you had, you'd be
in Windows by now. Instead, you're hunting for your Windows install disk, because
you're probably going to have to reinstall
your OS to get out of this one.

    Sounds kind of bad, doesn't it? Let's go ahead and prevent this agony and create a
password-reset disk. Click Start>Control Panel>User Accounts, then click your user account
name. Next, click the Prevent a Forgotten Password link under Related Tasks on the Tasks
Panel. This launches the Forgotten Password Wizard. Follow the directions for creating your
reset disk. Now, if you forget your password, you'll only be hunting down your reset disk not
the Windows install disk.

 WHAT'S THE PROCESS?

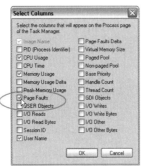

When an error occurs in Windows, the first place you should look for answers is in the Windows Task Manager. When you have a problem, check your Processes. Press Ctrl-Alt-Delete to launch the Task Manager, then click the Processes tab. The info listed here is fairly useful—you can check your CPU and memory usage for running programs—but what you may not be aware of is that you can get additional statistics on the Processes page. Click View>Select Columns on the Menu Bar, now check whatever additional details you want to add, then click OK. My personal favorites are Page Faults and Peak Memory Usage. These details can offer an enormous amount of info to help you identify problems.

 SPECIAL EVENTS

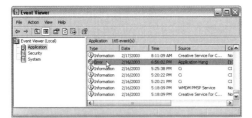

Every time an error occurs in Windows, it's saved. These error records are extremely valuable when troubleshooting problems—they actually make sense. You can view these records by clicking Start>Control Panel>Performance and Maintenance> Administrative Tools>Event Viewer. Windows saves errors in three Log Files: Application, Security, and System. Click any of the three Log Files to view saved errors in the appropriate pane. Now when you have a problem, make note of the date and time the error occurred, then check the Event Viewer for errors that were saved at the same time. Most recorded events are informational, but pay close attention to "Error" and "Warning" entries. Once you identify the correct error entry, use its information to search Microsoft's Knowledge Base for help.

I'M A NETWORK GURU

Have you ever had a problem with your computer's network connections? Did you feel completely helpless? Of course you did. You have no idea where to begin to figure out a networking problem. We're not supposed to understand this stuff—networking problems are for engineers and IT personnel. Well, actually there's a little-known tool in Windows that can help you discover exactly what your network problem is.

The next time you lose connectivity to the Internet or your network, click Start> All Programs>Accessories>System Tools> System Information, then click Tools>Net Diagnostics on the Menu Bar. Next, click the Scan Your System link. The scan pings your DNS servers, SMTP and POP3 mail servers, and gateways; checks your modems and network adapters; and provides a ton of other network info.

So next time you have a network problem, you can go to your IT person and say, "I'm not receiving a reply from the DHCP server or my Inbound Mail server when I ping them. It's probably a problem with my network adapter. Could you get on that as soon as you get a chance?" Then just turn and walk away, knowing that the guy's jaw just hit the floor. It's always fun stickin' to the IT guy!

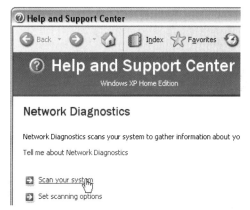

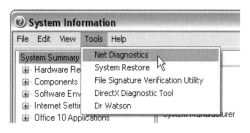

Feeling
Fearless?

WINDOWS XP
REGISTRY HACKS

WARNING! CAUTION! 911! Got your attention? Good! This chapter is for what I would consider advanced users of

Feeling Fearless?

windows xp registry hacks

Windows XP. Do not attempt any of these tips unless you know and completely understand what you're doing. Just like I would never *dip myself in honey and run naked through a killer bee farm, I would* never *joke around about Windows Registry. It's mean, it's nasty, and it will make you cry. There's nothing worse than booting up to a blank, gray screen. I've seen it happen, and, yes, they cried. So, if you're not familiar with Windows Registry, if you've never seen, much less used, Registry Editor, or if you feel uncomfortable in any way editing your Registry, then close the book...you're finished. I hope you enjoyed it.*

Okay, the warning's over. Are you still with me? Alright! Let's get to it. This chapter has some of my favorite and most popular Registry hacks. So, enjoy! And, oh yeah, be careful! I'm not kidding—they actually cried!

 BACK UP YOUR REGISTRY

This is your official warning: Back up your Windows Registry before making any changes to it. There are several ways to back up your Registry; however, the best is to use Backup. By default, the Windows Backup utility is not preinstalled on XP Home Edition, so you're going to have to install it. You can find it on your Windows XP Home Edition CD-ROM in the ValueAdd folder. Also, you should create a Restore Point. Again, do not make any changes to your Registry before backing it up. So, in case you're not quite getting it…back up your Registry. Okay? Okay!

 REGISTRY FAVORITES

Right off the bat, this is gonna save you a ton of time. Navigating Registry keys to find just the right attribute can take time and more than a few steps, but fortunately your Registry has its own Favorites. So, once you've finally arrived at your destination, click

Favorites on the Menu Bar, and then click Add to Favorites. Next, give your location a name and click OK. Now, any time you want to get back to that attribute, it's just one click away instead of 20.

I PREFER TRASH

By default, you can't rename the Recycle Bin. That stinks (no pun intended)! I really want to rename my Recycle Bin to Trash. It just makes more sense to me. Well, we've gotta do something about this.

To rename your Recycle Bin, click Start>Run, then type "regedit" (without quotes) in the dialog box, and click OK. This launches Windows Registry Editor. Navigate to "HKEY_CLASSES_ROOT\CLSID\{645FF040-5081-101B-9F08-00AA002F954E}\ShellFolder." Next, double-click Attributes in the right pane to open the Attributes dialog box. You'll see a data value of "0000 40 01 00 20." Highlight the 40, then change the 40 to 50 so that the Value Data looks like "0000 50 01 00 20," then click OK. Also, make certain that the Call for Attributes data value is

set to 0x00000000 (0), by double-clicking it and typing 0 (zero) as its Value Data if necessary. Now, right-click your Desktop and click Refresh on the Shortcut menu. Now right-click the Recycle Bin and you now have Rename as an option on the Shortcut menu. If you want to get rid of Rename on your Shortcut menu, change back the Attributes Value Data from 50 to 40.

 IT'S ALL IN THE NAME

Are you selling your computer or did your company just change names? Whatever the reason, you may actually need to update the registered owner of your system's OS eventually. Here's how: Open Registry Editor and navigate to HKEY_LOCAL_MACHINE\SOFTWARE\ Microsoft\Windows NT\CurrentVersion. In the right pane, double-click RegisteredOrganization. Now, type your new name in the Value Data text field in the dialog box then click OK. Repeat the process for RegisteredOwner.

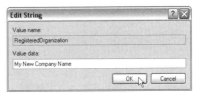

SPEEDIER MENUS

This is a hack I always use. Have you ever noticed the delay before the Start and All Programs menus expand. If you haven't, try it. See how it takes a second or two for the menu

to expand once you've pointed to it? Well, you can speed this up. Open Registry Editor and navigate to HKEY_CURRENT_USER\Control Panel\Desktop. Next, double-click MenuShowDelay in the right pane, and then change the Value Data to something like 100. Now, restart Windows and check out how much faster your menus are.

I DON'T NEED THE ARROWS

I extremely dislike (I can't say hate) shortcut arrows on my icons. It's just bad design, and they really annoy me. So, here's one of my personal favorites. Let's get rid of the arrows. Open Registry Editor and navigate to HKEY_CLASSES_ROOT\lnkfile, and rename the existing IsShortcut string value to IsShortcutOld. Now, restart Windows and the arrows are gone! If, for whatever crazy reason, you ever want them back, simply change the string value back to the original.

START WITHOUT ME

Do you know that it's you using your computer? If you don't, you can just look at the top of your Start menu and there you are. It's a good thing that Windows tells me that it's me using my computer, because sometimes I'm just not

sure. In case you can't tell I'm being sarcastic, I actually think that it's annoying that my user name appears on my Start Menu, so I'm going to remove it.

Open Registry Editor and navigate to HKEY_ CURRENT_USER\Software\Microsoft\Windows\ CurrentVersion\Policies\Explorer, and create a new DWORD Value in the Attributes Pane. To do this, right-click in the Attributes Pane, point to New, and click DWORD Value on the Shortcut menu, and then name it "NoUser-NameInStartMenu." Next, double-click your new attribute and give it a Value Data of 1 (0 = display user name, 1 = hide user name),

then click OK. If the NoNameInStartMenu value already exists, simply change the Value Data to 1. Restart Windows to view the change.

 I'VE GOT A TIP FOR YOU

This is actually pretty cool and a lot of fun. You can change Windows default tips to whatever you'd like. At my office, we change them to motivational remarks and cruel jokes about the hygiene of co-workers, but that's just us. I'm sure you can find your own uses for 'em.

Open Registry Editor and navigate to HKEY_LOCAL_MACHINE\SOFTWARE\Microsoft\Windows\CurrentVersion\Explorer\Tips. Now, simply double-click an existing String Value, replace the existing tip with one of your own in the Value Data text field, and then click OK. If you want to add new tips, just right-click in the Attributes Pane, point to New, and click String Value on the Shortcut menu. Number your new values in numerical order to the existing values, double-click the new value, type your tip into the Value Data text field, and then click OK. You now have new Windows tips.

 MY MEDIA PLAYER

I think I'm going to name Windows Media Player after me. Why not? I use it enough. Open Registry Editor and navigate to HKEY_CURRENT_USER\Software\Policies\Microsoft. Now, create a new Registry key: Right-click the Microsoft folder, Point to New, and click Key on the Shortcut menu. Now, name your new Key "Windows-MediaPlayer" (without quotes). Next, with the WindowsMediaPlayer key selected, right-click in the Attributes Pane (at right), point to New, and click String Value on the Shortcut menu. Name the new String Value "TitleBar" (without quotes). Now, double-click the TitleBar attribute, type any name you'd like in the Value Data text field, and click OK. Then, restart Windows and launch Media Player. Media Player has a new name. Your new text follows "Windows Media Player provided by" on the Title Bar.

OUTLOOK EXPRESS SHOULD START HERE

This is a cool hack—I don't know why it's cool, it just is. There's just something about being able to change programs in ways that you didn't know you could that's, well, just cool.

Open Outlook Express and click the Outlook Express icon in the Folders List. You see the default start page, right? Now, open Registry Editor or navigate to HKEY_CURRENT_USER\ Identities\"Your Identity"\Software\Microsoft\Outlook Express\5.0. Next, right-click in the Attributes Pane, point to New, and click String Value on the Shortcut menu. Name the new String Value "FrontPagePath"

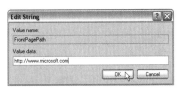

(without the quotes). Now, double-click the FrontPagePath attribute, type any URL you'd like in the Value Data text field, and click OK. Restart Windows and launch Outlook Express. Now, click the Outlook Express icon in the Folders List and your Web page will be displayed instead of the default start page.

 CONTROL THE CONTROL PANEL

Do you want to keep users from changing settings in the Control Panel? Heck, do you want to keep users from even being able to access the Control Panel? You can do that. Here's how: Open Registry Editor and navigate to HKEY_LOCAL_ MACHINE\SOFTWARE\Microsoft\Windows\

CurrentVersion\policies\Explorer. If you don't see the Explorer Key (folder), then create it under policies. Here's how: Right-click "policies," then click New>Key on the Shortcut menu, and name the new key "Explorer." Next, create a new DWORD Value by right-clicking on the Attributes Pane on the right, point to New, and click DWORD Value on the Shortcut menu. Then name it "NoControlPanel." Next, double-click the new DWORD Value,

type 1 in the Value Data text field, then click OK. Now, try to access tools in your Control Panel. You can't, can you? Cool! To get your Control Panel back, simply change the Value Data to 0 (zero). *Note:* You may have to restart Windows for the changes to take effect.

HACK IE'S TITLE BAR

Did you know that you can customize Internet Explorer's Title Bar with your company name, slogan, or whatever? Well, you can—if you hack it. This actually offers a nice touch when giving browser-based presentations to clients. It's also great for simply personalizing your browser.

Open Registry Editor and navigate to HKEY_CURRENT_USER\Software\Microsoft\Internet Explorer\Main. Next, right-click in the Attributes Pane, point to New, then click String Value on The Shortcut menu. Name the new String Value "WindowTitle" (without quotes). Now, double-click the new WindowTitle attribute, type any name you'd like in the Value Data text field, and click OK. Launch Internet Explorer, and your text will appear in IE's Title Bar (you may have to restart Windows). To get back the default IE Title Bar, simply delete the WindowTitle attribute.

 HOW ABOUT OUTLOOK EXPRESS' TITLE BAR?

I just love branding my programs with my company name, so let's keep the fun going and hack Outlook Express' Title Bar as well. Open Registry Editor and navigate to HKEY_CURRENT_USER\Identities\"Your Identity"\Software\Microsoft\Outlook Express\5.0. Next, right-click in the Attributes Pane, point to New, then click String Value on the Shortcut menu. Name the new String Value "WindowTitle" (without quotes). Now, double-click the new WindowTitle attribute, type any name you'd like in the Value Data text field, and click OK. Then, launch Outlook Express to view your new Title Bar (you may have to restart Windows). To get back the default Outlook Express Title Bar, simply delete the WindowTitle attribute.

FRIENDLY TREES AREN'T FRIENDLY AT ALL

Windows Explorer does something that I find to be very annoying. It uses Friendly Trees (auto-expanding folders). Sounds harmless, doesn't it? But, here's the problem with Friendly Trees. Basically, the term Friendly Trees refers to the way that an entire folder or directory expands when you click on them in Explorer's Folders Panel. Doesn't the folder already open in the right pane of Explorer? Yeah, it does. Well, maybe it's just me, but this just makes everything look unnecessarily cluttered. Let's make Windows Explorer truly friendly.

Open Registry Editor and navigate to HKEY_CURRENT_ USER\Software\Microsoft\Windows\CurrentVersion\Explorer\ Advanced. Next double-click the FriendlyTree binary string, change the Value Data to 0 (zero), then click OK. Now, launch Windows Explorer and click any folder. It didn't expand, did it? To get your Friendly Trees back, simply change the Value Data back to 1.

YOU'VE BEEN INFECTED

Want to really freak somebody out? Display a message when Windows starts up. This could be any message; for example, "Your computer has been infected with a virus. Your Hard Drive will automatically be reformatted in 10 seconds!" Now, when they fire up Windows, just sit back and watch the best 10-second display of panic you've ever seen. Or instead, you could just remind that special someone that you're thinking of them. They're both good.

Anyway, open your Registry Editor and navigate to HKEY_LOCAL_MACHINE\SOFTWARE\Microsoft\Windows NT\CurrentVersion\Winlogon. Next, double-click LegalNoticeCaption in the right pane, type a caption name in the Value Data text field for the Message dialog box, then click OK. Now, double-click LegalNoticeText, type the message you want to appear, and then click OK. Restart Windows.

     YOU CAN'T NOTIFY ME

This is for people who truly can't stand icons in their Taskbar Notification area. And I know you're out there. This hack will remove every single icon, not just hide them. They're gone! They're outta here!

You'll never be notified of another single thing.

Open Registry Editor and navigate to HKEY_LOCAL_MACHINE/SOFTWARE/Microsoft/Windows/CurrentVersion/policies/Explorer. If you don't see the Explorer Key (folder), then create it under policies. Here's how: Right-click "policies," then click New> Key on the Shortcut menu, and name the new key "Explorer." Next, create a new DWORD Value: Right-click on the Attributes Pane on the right, point to New, and click DWORD Value on the Shortcut menu. Next, name the value "NoTrayItemsDisplay" (without quotes), double-click the new attribute, type 1 in the Value Data text field, and then click OK. Now, restart Windows. To get your Notification icons back, simply change the Value Data to 0 (zero). *Note:* You may have to restart Windows for the changes to take effect.

GROUPING, MY WAY

The new Taskbar
Grouping feature
in XP is great for
keeping things from
getting out of hand
on the Taskbar; only
you can't change
how many similar
windows should be
allowed to be open

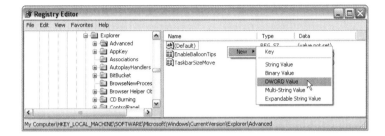

before the Taskbar groups 'em. Grouping happens dy-
namically depending on your display's resolution, which
is nice, but I want to be able to tell Windows when to
group buttons. I'm a control freak—it's a problem. So,
let's get pushy.

Open Registry Editor and navigate to HKEY_LOCAL_
MACHINE\SOFTWARE\Microsoft\Windows\CurrentVersion\
Explorer\Advanced. Next, create a new DWORD Value by
right-clicking on the Attributes Pane, point to New, and
click DWORD Value on the Shortcut menu. Name the value "TaskbarGroupSize" (without
quotes), double-click the new attribute, type a number, and then click OK. (I like five,
but that's just me.) Restart Windows. Now, your similar windows will automatically group
when five are opened.

Simply delete this attribute to return to the Windows default setting.

 "SHORTCUT TO" NOWHERE

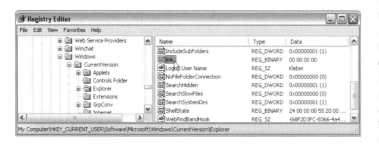

This is one of my all-time favorite Registry hacks. When you create a shortcut in Windows, not only does it come complete with the shortcut arrow, but its name also automatically begins with "Shortcut to." I think we all get that it's a shortcut. We just made it. Anyway, the first thing I do is delete the "Shortcut to" from the file's name, which automatically removes the "Shortcut to" text from your shortcuts when they're created.

Open Registry Editor and navigate to HKEY_CURRENT_USER\Software\Microsoft\Windows\CurrentVersion\Explorer. Next, double-click Link in the Attributes Pane (on the right). If you don't see the Link attribute, then create it. Here's how: Right-click in the right Attributes Pane and click New>Binary String on the Shortcut menu, then name the new value "link."

If the Link Attribute is already present, you'll see a Value Data of "0000 1E 00 00 00." Highlight the 1E, change the 1E to 00 so that the Value Data looks like "0000 00 00 00 00," then click OK. Now, restart Windows and create a shortcut. The "Shortcut to" text isn't there. That's much better! To get your shortcut text back, simply modify the Value Data back to "1E 00 00 00."

NOT-SO-RECENT DOCUMENTS

Use this hack to
automatically clear
your Recent Docu-
ments folder each
time that Windows is
shut down. This will
keep any unwanted
users from knowing
what you've been
up to. Maybe you're

really paranoid. Either way, open Registry Editor and
navigate to HKEY_LOCAL_MACHINE\SOFTWARE\Microsoft\
Windows\CurrentVersion\policies\Explorer. If you don't see
the Explorer Key (folder), then create it under policies.
Here's how: Right-click "policies," then click New>Key
on the Shortcut menu, and name the new key "Explorer."

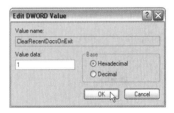

Next, create a new DWORD Value by right-clicking on the Attributes Pane, pointing to New,
and clicking DWORD Value on the Shortcut menu. Name the value "ClearRecentDocsOnExit"
(without quotes). Now, double-click the new attribute, type the number 1 for the Value
Data, then click OK. Now, restart Windows. When Windows launches, your Recent Documents folder is empty. To keep your recent documents, simply change the Attribute Value
Data to 0 (zero). *Note:* You may have to restart Windows for the changes to take effect.

WHO ARE YOU?

Do you want to rename My Computer to your user name and computer name? Sure you do. Actually this is helpful, especially if you

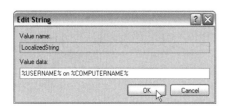

work from different workstations and need to quickly identify which computer you're working at and the user who's currently logged on.

Open Registry Editor and navigate to HKEY_CLASSES_ROOT\CLSID\{20D04FE0-3AEA-1069-A2D8-08002B30309D}. Double-click the "LocalizedString" Attribute in the right pane, highlight and copy the existing Value Data, and save this string in case you want to reset the attribute to its default setting. Next, replace the existing Value Data text

Kleber on
KLEBER

with "%USERNAME% on %COMPUTERNAME%" (without quotes) and then click OK. Now, right-click your Desktop and click Refresh on the Shortcut menu. When you restart, your user name and computer name will now be displayed under the My Computer icon.

NO ACCESS

With this hack, you can prevent users from opening specific programs. Maybe you want to keep Solitaire all to yourself, or you don't want the kids to use Internet Explorer. Well, here's how to keep 'em out. There are two parts to this hack, so follow along carefully.

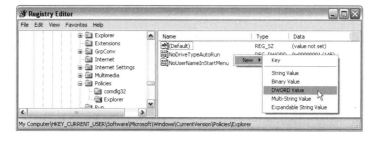

First, open Registry Editor and navigate to HKEY_CURRENT_USER\Software\Microsoft\Windows\CurrentVersion\Policies\Explorer. Then, create a new DWORD Value by right-clicking on the Attributes Pane (on the right), point to New, and click DWORD Value on the Short-cut menu. Name the value "DisallowRun" (without quotes). Now,

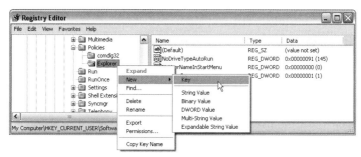

double-click the new attribute, type the number 1 for the Value Data, and then click OK. This enables application restrictions.

Next, right-click the Explorer key (folder) on the left, point to New, and click Key on the Shortcut menu. Name the new Key (folder) "DisallowRun" (without quotes). Then, click the new DisallowRun Key to open it. Right-click on the Attributes Pane, point to New, and click String Value. Name the new String Value using the number 1. Now, double-click the new String Value, type the applications name (e.g. notepad.exe), then click OK.

To add additional programs, simply number them consecutively, along with the Apps name as the Value Data. Restart Windows and try to launch Notepad. You can't.

 HYPER-TRASH

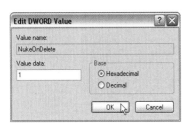

It's time to get serious about the Trash. This hack will delete files *immediately*, bypassing the Recycle Bin. If you use the Shift-Delete shortcut to bypass the Recycle Bin to delete files quickly and permanently, then this is the perfect timesaving tip.

Open Registry Editor and navigate to HKEY_LOCAL_ MACHINE\SOFTWARE\Microsoft\Windows\CurrentVersion\ Explorer\BitBucket. Next, double-click the Attribute NukeOnDelete, change the Value Data to 1, and then click OK. Now, when you delete a file it's really gone. Restart Windows to start using your new hyper-trash.

You can get back your default delete by changing back the NukeOnDelete Value Data to 0 (zero).

INDEX

A

Adobe Type Manager (ATM), 117
Address Bar. *(See Internet)*
Address Toolbar. *(See Toolbars)*
Advanced Tag Editor.
(See Media Player 9)
All Programs, 32, 74, 113, 122, 212
animations. *(See also Desktop)*
archive Web page, 160
AutoMovie. *(See under MovieMaker 2)*

B

background. *(See Desktop)*
Blue Screen of Death, 232
Briefcase, 46

C

CD
   file size, 233
CD Player, 217
Character Map, 98
ClearType, 125
clock, 45, 124
compatibility.
   (See Help and Support Center)
compressed files, 10, 60
contacts. *(See e-mail)*
Control Panel, 5, 245
cursors, 51
custom characters, 120

D

delete, *(See also Recycle Bin)*
   62, 90, 100, 104, 212
Desktop, 42
   animations, 50-51
   background, 46-47, 166
   icons, 218
   themes, 48
   Quick Launch, 94
   Web pages on Desktop, 48-50

Details Pane, 24
Details view. *(See views)*
Disk Cleanup, 226
Disk Defragmenter, 227
Document Scrap, 112

E

e-mail, 171-195
   attachments, 91, 188
   Bcc, 175
   Block Sender, 185
   contacts, 175, 178, 186-189
   Inbox, 173
   fonts, 184
   group, 174
   Hide Read Messages, 184
   Message Pane, 176
   Messenger, 190-195, 216
   new mail rules, 177, 185
   notification, 172, 186
   Preview Pane, 188
   Read Receipt, 179
   save, 182
   Signature, 179
   Spell options, 183
   startup, 172
   status, 216
   stationery, 180-181
   subject, 176
   To Do, 181
   vCard, 189
equalizer. *(See Media Player 9)*
error
   copy dialog box, 231
   Log Files, 236
   Processes, 236
   reporting, disable, 213
Escape, 104
Explorer.
   (See Internet and Windows Explorer)

F

Favorites, 37, 92-93
fax, 115

file(s),
   create 123
   compressed 10, 60
   delete, 62, 104
   explore, 55-56
   extensions, 68-69, 129
   full name, 85
   group, 59
   hide, 60, 219
   move, 56, 70, 102-103
   open multiple, 94
   open with, 100
   rename, 90-91
   save, 65-68, 233
   search, 107
   Send To, 118
   sort, 58
Filmstrip. *(See views)*
folders
   create, 83
   delete, 100
   hide, 123, 219
   icons, 79, 119
   move, 74
   Properties, 99
   private, 126
   rename, 110
   search, 107
   select, 86-87
   templates, 20
fonts, 116-117, 184
Friendly Trees. *(See Registry Editor)*

G

Games, 114
Go, 62
group, 59, 174

H

hack. *(See Registry Editor)*
Help. *(See also Remote Assistance)*
   save pop-ups, 122
Help and Support Center
   Favorites, 229
   Microsoft Knowledge Base, 225
   Program Compatibility Wizard, 227

Photoshop® 7 with a Wacom® Tablet

Photoshop's behind-the-scenes photo editing power...

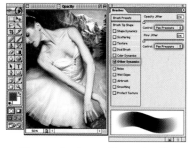

1. Dynamically change tool size

A Wacom pen tablet gives you the power to change the size of any of Photoshop's 20 pressure-sensitive tools with pen pressure. Press softly to get a thin stroke–press harder to get a thicker stroke. Here's the Clone Stamp set up to be pressure-sensitive for size–try out the other pressure-sensitive tools for fun! *(Visit our web site for a list of all 20 pressure-sensitive Photoshop tools.)*

2. Change tool opacity on the fly

Set the Paintbrush for Opacity, and you have Photoshop's most powerful tool for great layer masks! *Paint lightly for a semi-transparent look, press harder for a clean knock-out. And when you're done with your Layer Mask, give the Art History brush a try–press lightly with your pen for transparent strokes, press harder for more opaque strokes.*

3. Blend colors with your Paintbrush

Being able to change color during a brush stroke can give you some great effects. Set the Photoshop 7 Paintbrush to be color-sensitive in the Color Dynamics sub-palette, and try it out. We've set the Paintbrush to be color-sensitive for an "organic" look as we colorize the black & white photo below with two different shades of peach.

4. Try a little tilt

Select the Shape Dynamics sub-palette, and you can set the Angle to be affected by Pen Tilt. Modify a round brush to be an angular calligraphy brush, tilt the pen to the left or right, and you'll get beautiful calligraphic brushstrokes. *(By the way, almost all of the pressure-sensitive tools are tilt-sensitive too!)*

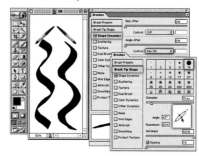

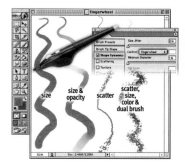

5. A finger on the Wacom Airbrush

Wacom's Airbrush Pen now offers you new method of control in Photoshop 7–th Fingerwheel. Grab the Wacom Airbrush, sele the Photoshop Paintbrush, and you can set size opacity, scatter, color, and more to respond to th roll of the fingerwheel.

6. The comfort you need

The Intuos2 Grip Pen is built for comfort. It ha a cushioned, contoured grip area and feature Wacom's patented cordless, battery-free technology for a natural feel and superior performance.

7. Put it all together

Now imagine editing photographs with som of your favorite Photoshop techniques and th Wacom tablet. Control size and opacity wi pressure to create accurate layer masks, burn ar dodge quickly, and make subtle color correctior exactly where you want them.

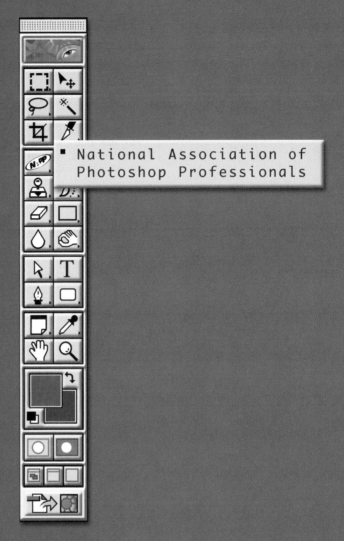

The only tool you need to master Adobe Photoshop

If you use Photoshop, you know that it's never been more important to stay up to date with your Photoshop skills as it is today. That's what the National Association of Photoshop Professionals (NAPP) is all about, as we're the world's leading resource for Photoshop training, education, and news. If you're into Photoshop, you're invited to join our worldwide community of Photoshop users from 106 different countries around the world who share their ideas, solutions, and cutting-edge techniques. Join NAPP today—it's the right tool for the job.

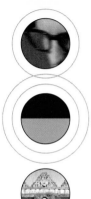

HOW TO CONTACT US

VISIT OUR WEB SITE

WWW.NEWRIDERS.COM

On our Web site you'll find information about our other books, authors, tables of contents, indexes, and book errata. You will also find information about book registration and how to purchase our books.

EMAIL US

Contact us at this address: **nrfeedback@newriders.com**

- If you have comments or questions about this book
- To report errors that you have found in this book
- If you have a book proposal to submit or are interested in writing for New Riders
- If you would like to have an author kit sent to you
- If you are an expert in a computer topic or technology and are interested in being a technical editor who reviews manuscripts for technical accuracy

- To find a distributor in your area, please contact our international department at this address. **nrmedia@newriders.com**

- For instructors from educational institutions who want to preview New Riders books for classroom use. Email should include your name, title, school, department, address, phone number, office days/hours, text in use, and enrollment, along with your request for desk/examination copies and/or additional information.
- For members of the media who are interested in reviewing copies of New Riders books. Send your name, mailing address, and email address, along with the name of the publication or Web site you work for.

BULK PURCHASES/CORPORATE SALES

The publisher offers discounts on this book when ordered in quantity for bulk purchases and special sales. For sales within the U.S., please contact: Corporate and Government Sales (800) 382-3419 or **corpsales@pearsontechgroup.com**. Outside of the U.S., please contact: International Sales (317) 428-3341 or **international@pearsontechgroup.com**.

WRITE TO US

New Riders Publishing
800 East 96th Street, Suite 200
Indianapolis, IN 46240

CALL US

Toll-free (800) 571-5840. Ask for New Riders.
If outside U.S. (317) 428-3000. Ask for New Riders.

FAX US

(317) 428-3280

New Riders

WWW.NEWRIDERS.COM

VOICES THAT MATTER

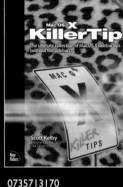
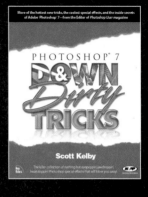
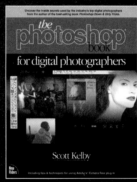